"Mom, *I hate my life!*"

"Peppered with examples from her counseling practice and her own experiences as a mother of a teenage girl, Hersh's book urges sensible compassion as mothers and daughters become companions on a mutual journey. She gives concrete and specific examples of how mothers can appropriately respond to their daughters' pain and help them understand their feelings. Throughout, Hersh also offers a central Christian message that God's love should be the foundation of girls' and mothers' identities."

—PUBLISHERS WEEKLY

"No one is more precious and disturbing to us than our children. There is no subject we are more desperate and fearful to enter than parenting. And there is no better book than *'Mom, I Hate My Life!'* to honestly and hopefully guide you to hope. We all know our children face realities we could never have imagined, and we rightfully need a wise, kind, and generous guide. Sharon Hersh lives and writes with brilliance, wisdom, and winsome wit. This book will allow you to encounter the rapids of your daughter's adolescence with greater confidence and joy."

—DAN ALLENDER, author of *How Children Raise Parents*

"The two greatest complaints I hear from teens about their parents are these: 'They don't listen, and they don't understand.' Sadly, those complaints are usually warranted. Sharon Hersh has once again done moms and daughters a great favor by providing a depth of understanding that can close the cultural-generational gap. No doubt our girls are in crisis. *'Mom, I Hate My Life!'* is a compelling cry that can help undo the crisis by challenging and equipping moms to meet their daughters' deepest needs in the best way possible. But this isn't just a book for moms. Dads, youth workers, and anyone else working with young girls will have their eyes opened to the painful realities of growing up female in today's world."

—WALT MUELLER, founder and president of the Center for Parent/Youth Understanding and author of *Understanding Today's Youth Culture*

"In an age where teens themselves struggle to put words to their own kaleido-scope of confusing emotions, this is a wonderful book for teen girls, parents, and counselors alike. I highly recommend it—it can save lives."

—CHRISTIAN HILL, parent and counselor, Alpine Connection Counseling

"Want to rebuild, restore, and refresh your relationship with your daughter? Countless moms and daughters will be blessed by this carefully crafted book. Sharon Hersh speaks hope into the mom-daughter relationship. You *can* have a trusting, rich relationship with your daughter—this book will show you how!"

—GREGORY L. JANTZ, PHD, author of *Moving Beyond Depression* and *Hope, Help, and Healing for Eating Disorders*

"Mom, *I hate my life!*"

Becoming your daughter's ally through the
emotional ups and downs of adolescence

sharon a. hersh

SHAW BOOKS

an imprint of WATERBROOK PRESS

"Mom, I Hate My Life!"
A SHAW BOOK
PUBLISHED BY WATERBROOK PRESS
2375 Telstar Drive, Suite 160
Colorado Springs, Colorado 80920
A division of Random House, Inc.

All Scripture quotations, unless otherwise indicated, are taken from *The Message.* Copyright ©
1993, 1994, 1995, 1996, 2000, 2001, 2002. Used by permission of NavPress Publishing Group.
Scripture quotations marked (AMP) are taken from *The Amplified® Bible,* Copyright © 1954,
1958, 1962, 1964, 1987 by the Lockman Foundation. All rights reserved. Used by permission.
(www.Lockman.org) Scripture quotations marked (KJV) are taken from the *King James Version.*
Scripture quotations marked (NIV) are taken from the *Holy Bible, New International Version®.*
NIV®. Copyright © 1973, 1978, 1984 by International Bible Society. Used by permission of
Zondervan Publishing House. All rights reserved.

Names and details in anecdotes and stories have been changed to protect the identities of the
persons involved.

ISBN 0-87788-023-9

Library of Congress Cataloging-in-Publication Data
Hersh, Sharon A.
  "Mom, I hate my life!" : becoming your daughter's ally through the emotional ups and downs
of adolescence / Sharon A. Hersh.—1st ed.
      p. cm.
  Includes bibliographical references.
  ISBN 0-87788-023-9
  1. Motherhood—Religious aspects—Christianity. 2. Mothers and daughters—Religious
aspects—Christianity. 3. Teenage girls—Conduct of life. I. Title.
BV4529.18 .H47 2004
248.8'431—dc22   2003022670

Printed in the United States of America
2004

10 9 8 7 6 5 4 3

To my friend Joan—Braveheart Mom

CONTENTS

ACKNOWLEDGMENTS

I didn't think I would write this book. Its assignment came during a painfully hard time in my life. Writing it was a gift—a gift from God and all the amazing people in my life who gave God a face.

Kristin and Graham—Thank you for sharing your stories and for being my greatest teachers. You demonstrate that you can hate things about your life and still live well, love faithfully, and laugh a lot.

My parents, John and Kathleen Baker—Thank you for continuing to father and mother me.

All my mother-daughter clients and teachers, including but not limited to the following—Amy and Amanda; Jessie and Josie; Ellen and Lauren; Linda and Jessie; Jill and Kate; Susan and Meg; Cami and Katie; Carol and Heather and Holly; Cindy and Danika; Debbie and Britney; Connie and Mallory; Jill and Mo; Megan and Meredith.

Publisher Don Pape and all the wonderful people at WaterBrook Press and Shaw Books—Your interactions consistently confirm that you all are about so much more than just business.

My editor-friend, Traci Mullins—I most certainly would not have written this book without you. Thanks for your insight, encouragement, and commitment, and for telling me, "Write."

A Haven in the Storm

My first vivid memory…is…when first I looked into her face and she looked into mine. That I do remember, and that exchanging look I have carried with me all my life. We recognized each other. I was her child and she was my mother….

What I inherited from my mother is inside me.

—PEARL S. BUCK, *Mothers*

When my daughter, Kristin, was in the fifth grade, I made the mistake of asking an unwelcome question. I thought I was gathering information, when in reality I was opening the door to a brewing storm.

"So, do you have any homework tonight?" I asked routinely after I picked her up from school.

"I don't know." Kristin's short, sullen answer did not invite further conversation, but I continued full speed ahead.

"Well, how about that English essay? Isn't it due this week?"

"Mom, I said I don't know."

"I just don't want you to wait until the last minute," I continued, ignoring Kristin's verbal and nonverbal cues that it was not a good moment for a time-management tip.

"Mom, I can't even think about schoolwork right now. Lindy and I had a big fight, and we aren't friends anymore. I hate her. Eric said my shoes looked like his grandmother's shoes, and everyone laughed. I hate boys. I don't have any friends. No one likes me. *I hate my life!*"

I summoned enough wisdom to drop the subject of the English essay, but I did not know how to respond to my daughter's avalanche of angst. We drove home in silence, I muttered something about dinner being in a few hours, and I prayed that everything would be better by dinnertime. And it was.

But Kristin's problems have not always easily resolved themselves with time. Friendships do break apart, and sometimes families do too. Teenagers live in an occasionally cruel, often hard-to-manage world, and even when circumstances are calm, teenage girls experience an internal world of unmanageable emotions at the whim of budding hormones and changing biology. Moodiness and melancholy go with the territory.

Nearly every day my telephone rings and I answer to hear the confused, anxious, and desperate voices of mothers on the other end of the line:

"My daughter yells at me all the time. She's angry. She seems to hate everyone, including herself."

"Katie ran away last night. We don't know where she is."

"Brittany comes home, goes straight to her room, turns on her CD player, and won't talk to anyone."

"My daughter is only ten, but she is so anxious that she can't go to school."

"I frequently hear my daughter throwing up in the bathroom. I keep asking her if she is sick, but she says she's fine and to leave her alone. I suffered from bulimia myself when I was a young woman, and I'm terrified that she's suffering the same way."

"Last night I caught my daughter cutting herself with a razor blade."

Statistics and stories alike confirm that today's girls are growing up in a stormy world and that they are hurting, angry, and afraid. The statistics are sobering. Teenage girls ages twelve to nineteen are the most victimized segment of the population.[1] By the time a girl is fifteen years old, she will have confronted realities that most of us never dreamed could exist when we were teenagers:

- sexual harassment and aggression from her peers, encouraged by the popular culture
- daily drug and alcohol use and abuse among classmates

- dangerous liaisons via high-tech connections
- the possibility of death at the hands of other teenagers

Add to this stormy climate the reality that by the time a girl is fifteen years old, her emotions may feel like a hurricane that is blowing out of control without warning or reason. When a scary external world and a chaotic internal world collide, the result is often overwhelming and confusing. The challenges for moms wanting to wisely support their daughters and guide them toward emotional maturity are greater than ever before!

While the statistics are startling, the stories are familiar, intersecting with almost every family in which there is a growing girl. Of course, we couldn't imagine when our daughters were cute baby girls that one day they would stonily stare us in the face and announce, "I hate my life." No one could predict that our happy, busy toddlers would one day spend hours alone in their rooms, listening to music we don't understand, brooding over dark thoughts that they keep to themselves. As we casually listened to our little girls' chatter, we never dreamed that one day they might not tell us anything. And we would have gasped in utter disbelief if anyone had suggested that our daughters might one day keep a pocketknife hidden in their bedroom dressers, take it out occasionally, and use it to carefully carve their arms and legs with indecipherable markings, in part to relieve the emotional pain she feels.

The world our girls are navigating is not just scarier than the world we grew up in, but the internal storms of adolescence today seem particularly intense. Mothers call me—a complete stranger—because they are desperate for someone to help. I recognize their hearts full of longing for their daughters, because I have felt the same desire for my own children. Whatever I have learned in graduate school and in my counseling practice is being eclipsed by what my children are teaching me.

Perhaps you picked up this book not because your daughter is in crisis, but because you are just starting to get glimpses of her world and her emotional responses, and you don't know how to enter her world with compassion and confidence. If we mothers are tempted to throw up our hands in despair the moment we enter our daughters' worlds, how can our daughters survive? This book is my unfolding answer.

As mothers, we can become our daughters' greatest allies in the midst of the inevitable and sometimes scary emotional turmoil of growing up female.

What I call hand-in-hand mothering begins with the conviction that as we stretch to meet our daughters' needs—learning in the midst of not knowing, and giving even when we don't feel like we have anything to give—we can experience personal transformation and guide our daughters toward emotional maturity.

If you have picked up this book because you are discouraged beyond words or feel as if your daughter's struggles have you in way over your head, take heart! The power of transformation *for you* lies in the midst of the storm! In essence, this is a book about personally experiencing emotional wholeness as we help our daughters grow up healthy and whole.

I will not be presenting a plan to overthrow culture and turn back the tide of increasingly disturbing statistics and stories about teenagers, but I do want to assure you that your daughter's emotional development can become the context for your own growth, and that the *relationship* you have with your daughter can be a haven in the storm for both of you. This book is about developing a relationship with your daughter that enables you to confront *together* the challenges of helping her develop emotional maturity. Yes, that means *together* you can face typical teenage moodiness, hostile or silent withdrawal, swirling anxiety and worry, and even self-destructive behaviors that may arise in the midst of emotional turmoil, and not only survive, but thrive!

If this sounds too good to be true, let me reassure you that hand-in-hand mothering is not rooted in your special skills or talents. Find a picture of your daughter right now. Take a good look at what God has entrusted to you. The gift of your daughter was not contingent on your parenting skills, your background, or your success in life. In unrestricted, unconditional love, God gave you a daughter and made you a mother! The God-given bond between you and your child was created to be a place of growth and safety—a haven in the storm.

The off-center, in-between stage of puberty and adolescence is a crucial time to guide your daughter in opening her heart to life. Emotional maturity includes having a personal identity, self-regard, and a positive approach to life. Emotional maturity is gained in the midst of pleasure and pain, doubt and faith, confusion and wisdom. It is developed in each moment of our scary, strange, ordinary, and sometimes stormy lives. You can become your daughter's ally as she develops in regard to what she believes not only about herself but also about her place in this world.

Becoming allies. It sounds good, doesn't it? In fact, since the events of September 11, 2001, we have discovered as a nation that allies are comforting and essential. An ally is one who knows the enemy, understands the battle, and is always ready to lend a hand. This book will help you be the most effective and powerful ally possible to your daughter in the midst of her emotional turmoil. And as you cement this bond with her, you will have the opportunity to experience the reality of God's promise: "Two are better than one, because they have a good return for their work" (Ecclesiastes 4:9, NIV).

In the chapters that follow, I want to help you build the framework for becoming your daughter's ally in four ways. First, you'll come to understand your own world and your own emotional development (in the context of mothering—or not). Second, you'll dive into your daughter's world and its inevitable emotional turmoil. Third, you'll uncover many ways to bridge your two worlds. Surprisingly, your daughter's mood swings, her expressions of hurt and frustration, and even her painful experiences can become the most powerful means to connect the two of you in a journey toward emotional maturity. Finally, you'll take a look at some of the serious obstacles that can keep you from becoming your daughter's ally and can even derail you and your daughter's relationship completely—scary subjects such as eating disorders, self-injury, teenage depression, and thoughts of suicide.

Throughout this book you will see sections titled "Just for You" and "Just for the Two of You." The questions and practical exercises and experiences in these sections are designed to help you address your own emotions, and then to inspire you to translate your discoveries and growth into walking hand in hand with your daughter. Don't feel pressured to answer all the questions or do all the exercises. You will want to pick and choose based on your daughter's age and current questions and struggles.

When your daughter exclaims or murmurs, "Mom, I hate my life!" don't despair. Her words are not the end of the story. In fact, they may be the beginning of a great adventure. My prayer is that the pages ahead will reenergize you with a vision of what is possible *between* you and your daughter and *for* you and your daughter. Hand-in-hand mothering is a transformational process in which the overwhelming and daily struggles become the context for emotional and spiritual growth—for both of you.

Part 1

Understanding Your Worlds

Sell everything and buy Wisdom! Forage for Understanding!...
Never walk away from Wisdom—she guards your life;
  love her—she keeps her eye on you.
Above all and before all, do this: Get Wisdom!
    Write this at the top of your list: Get Understanding!
Throw your arms around her—believe me, you won't regret it;
  never let her go—she'll make your life glorious.

—PROVERBS 4:5-8

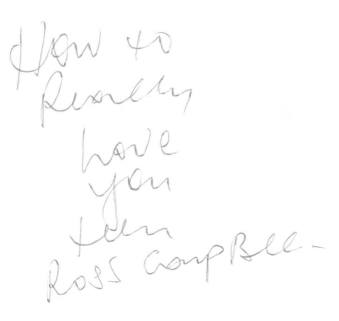

Being a Mom Is Not for the Faint of Heart

Motherhood is like Albania—you can't trust
the descriptions in the books, you have to go there.

—MARNI JACKSON, *The Mother Zone*

O
h no! It's somebody's mother!" A tall teenage boy peeked out the front door, looked at me, and then slammed the door yelling a warning to all inside.

I rang the doorbell a second time and thought about the events of the evening that had brought me to this house full of teenagers and apparently empty of parents.

Kristin, my sixteen-year-old daughter, had set out earlier in the evening to go to a movie. She called me from the theater to let me know that all the "good" movies were sold out and that she and a girlfriend were going to Dorrie's house.

"Who's Dorrie?" I asked.

"A girl in my biology class." The tone of Kristin's voice changed, and I could hear her defenses rising.

"Will Dorrie's parents be home?" I envisioned myself as a brilliant criminal defense lawyer collecting evidence to make my case.

"Yes, Mom." Kristin did not hide her contempt for my curiosity.

"Well, what are you going to do at Dorrie's house?"

"I don't know. We're just going to hang out. I've got to go, Mom. We're leaving."

During the course of this brief telephone conversation, Kristin's mood had gone from sweet cooperation to sour defiance. And my vision of myself had gone from savvy, good parent to timid, doormat mother.

"Just be home by eleven," I whimpered as we ended our conversation.

I knew I'd met my match and that Kristin was getting better and better at wielding her emotions like a cunning, sharp sword. I'm not saying that Kristin—a typical teenage girl with an emotional thermostat that can go from 0 to 120 degrees in a minute—is always in control of her emotional climate. She can wake up in the morning singing and full of sunshine and by 8:00 a.m. be sullen and withdrawn, threatening to storm any second. But she was learning to use this broad spectrum of emotions to her advantage.

Since my clinical work is primarily with adolescent girls and their mothers (and I remember being a moody teenager myself), I was not surprised to witness my own daughter's emotional life being tossed and turned by the biological and hormonal turmoil that comes with the territory of adolescence. What did surprise me was my own emotional instability in the face of Kristin's ever-changing internal state. When Kristin was sad, I felt down. When Kristin was irritable, I felt on edge. When Kristin was happy, all was well for me. When Kristin was angry or defensive, I felt afraid.

I had learned from my work with mothers and daughters that girls absorb the emotional maturity (or immaturity) of their mothers, and I knew that I needed to grow up. I knew that Kristin's stormy interior life needed a haven in my emotional response. I was challenged by the words of educators and therapists Harville Hendrix and Helen Hunt when they wrote:

> We take a step toward [maturity] when we understand our painful moments with our children can become a road map for our own healing journey. Follow the map, and we don't have to walk over the same broken ground over and over again. We can find a new path.[1]

GROWING YOURSELF UP

Mothering can move us toward emotional maturity as we help our daughters navigate the inevitable emotional turmoil of adolescence. This is not a journey, however, for the faint of heart. It's not always easy to look at ourselves honestly. It's especially hard to focus on our own growth and development when our children are in the midst of chaos. Although it is wholly appropriate for our daughters' struggles to show us where we need to grow and change, it is not appropriate for us to rely on our daughters to help us grow. They need to be absorbed in the full-time work of becoming themselves. Mothering can be lonely work.

Which brings us back to my story about Kristin, her trip to Dorrie's house, and my resemblance to the Cowardly Lion. I did a quick inventory of my fears in this particular context (we will examine the inventory process throughout this chapter and the next), took a few deep breaths, and prayed, *God, help me.* As I pulled away from Kristin's emotional state and settled into my own mother's heart, some things became clear to me. I knew that I had acquiesced to Kristin's request out of fear, not wisdom. I knew that I was growing to trust Kristin's choices in the midst of challenging teenage temptations, but I felt a sense of uneasiness about the unknown at Dorrie's house. As I let go of my fear of my daughter's defensiveness, I began to grab hold of my "mother's intuition." Intuition is a God-given sense that was designed to connect God's Spirit with our inner voice, and then in turn connect us to our children. Emotional immaturity disconnects us from our intuition.

My inner voice told me to go get my daughter. She had given me Dorrie's telephone number, and I plugged it into a specific Internet site that produced Dorrie's address. Since I am directionally dysfunctional, I sought further help from the Internet and got driving directions from a map Web site. I drove straight to Dorrie's house with a clear set of directions and a confident heart for my daughter.

I rang the doorbell a second time, and another tall teenage boy with that awkward mix of acne and facial hair answered the door. I calmly asked, "Would you please tell Kristin Hersh that her mother is here?"

Kristin came to the door, and her eyes met mine. The brief connection when our eyes met told me that I was reading the signals right. When we got into the car, Kristin's first words were, "How did you know?"

"How did I know what?" I asked.

"How did you know I needed you?"

Her next words burst with a description of the turbulent night she'd experienced. She explained that when they got to Dorrie's house, she discovered that the parents were not home. There were boys from another high school there, kids were drinking, and some were threatening to "fight." Kristin knew pretty quickly that she was in over her head, but she was uncertain as to how to extricate herself from the melee.

Kristin and I had a lot of conversations in the days ahead about making choices, staying true to her own values, and getting out while the getting is good. But this was not just an opportunity for me to confirm to my daughter that "mother knows best." Far more, this was an opportunity for me to confirm to myself that I do know some things and that I can and should rely on what I know.

WHY WE DON'T KNOW WHAT WE KNOW

We are born connected. Your daughter is an amazing gift, whether you carried her in your womb or she was first born in your heart and then came to you through adoption.

Can you remember when you looked at that mysterious and helpless bundle of baby for the first time? She needed you—depended on you for her very life. The giving required was almost entirely one way. God intended these demands of mothering to be transforming us while they arouse in us a keen sense of knowing for our children—knowing them, their needs, and our responsibility to be there for them, even when they're not there for themselves. Becoming a mother gives us the chance to live outside ourselves, to put aside our needs, and to think of the well-being of another.

An invisible thread connects those who are destined to meet, regardless of time and circumstance. The thread may stretch or tangle, but will never break.

—CHINESE LEGEND OF THE RED THREAD

How many times have you known when your daughter needed you before she even asked for help? When she was a baby, could you distinguish her cries for feeding from her cries for attention? Have you ever awakened in the middle of the night *knowing* that your daughter was in trouble or needed some specific direction from you?

Our "knowing" is the God-implanted instinct intended to be our compass during the inevitable storms of adolescence. But there is nothing like teenage turbulence to make us disregard our own internal compass while we grab on to the side of the rocking boat for dear life. We "drop our compass" most often when one of three waves of fear washes across our mother's heart: the "tapes" of the past, the troubles of the present, or the terrors of the future. These distortions of perspective slice through the connection with our daughters, weakening the invisible bond between us.

THE TAPES OF THE PAST

Child development researchers suggest that the most significant influence on how we parent is how we were parented as children.[2] A mother's emotional response to her daughter's emotional turmoil is shaped by her unique personal history. "It's almost as if we have 'parenting prints' on our brains in the same way that we have fingerprints on our fingers."[3] In the next chapter we will look more fully at your mothering style, but for now, read the following "Just for You" section to discover why that style came so naturally to you.

JUST FOR YOU

How you mother is often a reflection of how you were mothered. The following questions invite you to identify the "parenting print" you received from your mother. The purpose of these questions is not to "bash" your mom or to provide a pretext for blame, but to look at what was modeled to you and how you might want to change. Circle one answer for each of the following:

1. My mother expressed emotions in relation to herself (e.g., her fears, disappointments, desires, happiness or unhappiness).

   All of the time   Most of the time   Seldom   Never

2. My mother sacrificed her own needs, desires, and ambitions for me.

   All of the time   Most of the time   Seldom   Never

(continued on the following page)

3. My mother forgot about me or seemed distracted.

   All of the time   Most of the time   Seldom   *Never*

4. My mother "took over" for me (i.e., did my work, met my needs, took on my consequences, etc.).

   All of the time   Most of the time   Seldom   *Never*

5. My mother criticized, mocked, or rejected me.

   All of the time   Most of the time   Seldom   *Never*

6. My mother seemed overwhelmed by the demands of mothering.

   All of the time   Most of the time   Seldom   Never

7. My mother balanced my needs and life with her own needs and life.

   All of the time   Most of the time   Seldom   *Never*

Look at your circled answers above. On the basis of these answers, complete the following sentence, using one of the words below or a word of your own: My mom was most often _SELFLESS_ _SACRIFICAL_ in her parenting of me.

Self-absorbed	Critical	Rejecting	Smothering
Distant	Attentive	Overwhelmed	Confident
Distracted	Nurturing	Sacrificial	Anxious

Your mom is, of course, multidimensional, and your response to the sentence above does not completely define your mother, but it may help you begin to understand what you experienced as a child and how you might pass similar experiences on to your children.

Complete the following sentence using one of the words listed above or your own word: When my daughter is in emotional turmoil, I am most often _anxious_ in my parenting of her.

Were you surprised by your "parenting print" and how it has imprinted your mothering? As I embarked on the journey of growing myself up, I was able to identify my own mother's anxiety in her parenting of me, my inheritance of her anxiety, and my tendency to "default" to that style of mothering. When Kristin petulantly asked to go to Dorrie's house, I immediately retreated into fear—my fear of Kristin's anger and my fear of all that lurked at Dorrie's house—in part because that's how my mother parented me. My anxiety disconnected me from my heart for my daughter.

In the next chapter we will continue an inventory of our mothering styles, but as you embark on a journey to help your daughter navigate the inevitable emotional turmoil of adolescence, it's important for you to understand what has been modeled to you so far in your own journey. If you're at all like me, you want to take this growing awareness and change completely and immediately. But the journey to emotional maturity is not a quick trip for us or our daughters. Awareness is the first step. As you become increasingly aware of the impact of your own mother on you and your often unconscious similar mothering of your daughter, you have the opportunity to wake up. Hand-in-hand mothering is possible when we are awake—conscious of our own deficits and strengths, tendencies and possibilities.

An interesting transition occurs naturally and spontaneously when we are willing to look at ourselves honestly: As we become aware of ourselves, we may actually forget ourselves and begin to mother with courage and confidence. That is what it means to grow up.

THE TROUBLES OF THE PRESENT

It was a mother who first crooned, "Nobody knows the troubles I've seen." Perhaps you've picked up this book because you identify with the soulful words of that old spiritual. The following excerpt reflects one mother's growing awareness of the trials and travail of mothering:

> There were things that started to happen. But then you don't know. When your daughter is eleven, when your daughter starts to act different.... You don't know if it's because her mother works too much, or

because your daughter is too smart for her classes, or because she has maybe a learning disability you never caught, or because her teacher has a learning disability or isn't smart enough to teach your daughter. Or maybe it doesn't have anything to do with school at all. Maybe she is becoming a teenager and this is how they act. Maybe they are supposed to be quiet like this and stay up in their room.

And then something happens and you think: I think there's something wrong....

All of a sudden it just happens.

It seems like all of a sudden it just happens....

And then it seems as if it's happening all of the time now, ever since [she] started edging into adolescence.

And then it seems as if... It has been so long since someone hasn't been mad or exhausted or sad.[4]

No matter how many books we read on adolescent development, we are almost always surprised when our daughters are the moody ones, the sullen ones, the ones in their rooms with their music blaring. When something goes wrong with our daughters, it is normal for us to become afraid. Tumultuous times can paralyze us. When we allow the inevitable emotional turmoil our daughters are experiencing to overwhelm and engulf us in a wave of fear, we drown out the wisdom of our mother's heart.

More often than not, we are overwhelmed by present troubles when we have an unrealistic expectation of control. Our daughters' unpredictable emotional state becomes an invitation for us to examine our expectation of control and the resulting controlling tendencies. We give up control and get a grip on our fear when we remember two important principles for hand-in-hand mothering: Our daughters are not us, and we are not God.

OUR DAUGHTERS ARE NOT US

When our daughters are in trouble, it is essential for us to remember that we are separate beings. This can be hard for mothers because of our invisible bond with our daughters. The strength of our connection, however, is weakened when we perceive our daughters' struggles and failures as *our* struggles and failures. When my feelings, my questions, and my fears take over, I lose the capacity to mother from a wise and centered reality that is curious about my daughter and compassionate toward her struggles. Growing girls are moody and uncommunicative. That's natural. When we become moody in response, we are hampered in our ability to communicate to our daughters the messages that will help them grow toward emotional maturity.

When Kristin became defiant and contemptuous about going to Dorrie's house, I became cowardly and ineffective. I couldn't ask good questions or set healthy limits because I was stuck in my own emotional quagmire. I allowed Kristin to pull me into this muck because I didn't stop to separate myself from her. I forgot what I knew about teenage gatherings and what I needed to offer Kristin even if she didn't want it.

The bond with our daughters can seem more like a yoke when we don't separate in healthy and wise ways.

In the following chapters we will look more closely at your emotional

JUST FOR YOU

Complete the following sentences when you feel overwhelmed in relationship with your daughter:

1. When my daughter is angry, I feel _____.
2. When my daughter withdraws, I feel _____.
3. When my daughter is sad, I feel _____.
4. When my daughter's mood changes, my own mood
   _____.

5. How often does your own mood mirror your daughter's?

   All of the Time   Most of the Time   Seldom   Never

Complete the following sentences:

1. When my daughter is angry, I would like to feel _____.
2. When my daughter withdraws, I would like to feel _____.
3. When my daughter is sad, I would like to feel _____.
4. When my daughter's mood changes, I would like my own mood
   to _____.

response to your daughter's emotional turmoil. Right now a growing awareness of where you stop and your daughter begins is the goal.

WE ARE NOT GOD

We get lost in our daughters' emotional turmoil not only when we lose our
perspective about ourselves but also when we lose our perspective about God.
We mothers often want to believe we are more powerful and loving than God
is. We hold on to unrealistic expectations for our children when we forget
that God is in control and act as if we are.

Psalm 46:1 describes God's response to our trouble as "very present"
(KJV). God is of course omnipresent, and we mothers are not. But I don't
think this description of God is only about His omnipresence; it is also about
His personal presence. Sometimes God's only response to our troubles is to
be present. When we are consumed with the desire to fix our daughters or to
control them, we lose the ability to be present, to be with our daughters in
the midst of the storm.

JUST FOR YOU

Consider praying the following prayer: *God, I release my daughter to Your
care. I trust You to be with her and me in the midst of turmoil.*

1. What, if anything, keeps you from praying these words with complete
   trust and relinquishment?
2. What does this prayer suggest you believe about God?
3. What is the significance of surrendering your daughter to the *care*
   of God?
4. Consider praying these words every morning and evening.

THE TERRORS OF THE FUTURE

Just as our tapes of the past and the troubles of the present can weaken our
connection with our daughters, so can our anxiety about the future. There is
of course a natural link between trouble in the present and fear of the future.
You can be sure my intervention for Kristin at Dorrie's house was propelled
by fleeting and fearful thoughts not only about the immediate threats to

Kristin's well-being but also about the looming possibility of her being assaulted, dropping out of high school, working as a bartender, and living in a dangerous part of town with no furniture and a bare light bulb as her only source of warmth and lighting. Yes, I thought about all that.

In [one] category are the mothers who have "easy" children.
These children keep their rooms tidy without being asked. They even
offer to set the table. Some kids are born that way, meaning it's their
natural predisposition to veer toward compliance and responsibility.
Watch out for the mother of such a child, especially if she takes full
credit for the child's behavior.

—HARRIET LEARNER, *The Mother Dance*

What I am learning as I have the privilege of working with mothers and daughters is that we cannot predict our children's futures. Girls who grow up in wonderful families with abundant resources make foolish mistakes that derail their life courses and often deepen their wisdom and faith along the path of hard consequences. And girls who grow up in difficult family situations with little support often become amazing, insightful young women at a young age—probably due, in part, to their less than desirable life circumstances.

So stop worrying. Of course, it's ridiculous to tell mothers not to worry. The toughest emotional challenge of mothering is to get a grip on our anxiety. It is important to note that not all mothers *feel* anxious. Anxiety can be cloaked in a number of disguises. Control, disgust, manipulation, detachment, and anger are all manifestations of anxiety that our beautiful baby girl is growing into someone (or something) we can't manage. The premise of this book is that our emotional life is important and that our emotions can teach us a lot; but when we are ignorant of our own emotions and their roots, they often grow into an unattractive and unruly garden that can choke out our own inner voice of wisdom as well as the coaching of God's Spirit.

The same psalm that tells us God is present reminds us that we must be *still* to experience the benefits of His presence. When you find your heart filled with anxiety about the future and your mind racing with improbable possibilities, stop. Remind yourself that it is normal for mothers to worry and that you are not in control—God is.

Often our worries about the future are colored by our need for everything to look okay. I knew that when my imagination envisioned a scantily clad Kristin living in a seedy neighborhood and working in a questionable profession, my fear was being fueled by my need for everything to look good. Children are wonderful teachers, and one of the things they definitely teach us is

Just for You

Worrying and mothering often go hand in hand. If we want to walk hand in hand with our daughters in navigating the inevitable emotional turmoil that comes with adolescence, we must develop the practice of being still. This practice is not about holding it all in until you can explode later or developing a Pollyannaish sense of denial. It is about letting go (since we're not in control anyway) and letting God be with us along the way.

Remember that the ruts of worry and anxiety probably run deep in our hearts and minds from lots of travel over the same road. We have to carve new grooves by a persistent sojourn along new pathways.

Try the following meditation as many times during the day (or night) as possible.

- When circumstances cause emotional upheaval—whether big or small—describe your internal life in detail to God. Describe the worry, anger, disgust, detachment, or numbness as well as the specifics of this trigger for the emotional turmoil.
- Don't attach sentences to your prayer such as *God, make this go away,* or *God, make me not feel this.* We shortchange our relationship with God when we make Him a vending machine for our emotional woes, hoping we'll put in a prayer and He'll give us what we tell Him to.
- Invite God into true relationship by asking Him to be present in the midst of your troubles.
- Be still. One of the best physical exercises that can aid this spiritual state is to take five slow, deep breaths—*deep* breaths from your belly. And slowly release each breath while you pray, *God, not my will, but Yours be done.*

that we mothers care a lot about good form and appearances, which may result in our own agendas overriding the needs of our children.

This is a good time to apply an irrefutable principle of physics and emotions: Reactivity breeds reactivity. When we are filled with fear, we breed anxiety in our children. When our worry is fueled by concern about form over substance, we send the wrong message to our children: that looking good is more important than growing. When we are angry, we birth hostility or smoldering resentment in our daughters. When we are controlling, our daughters may feel out of control or smothered. When we are disgusted with our adolescent girls' awkward and inevitably messy growth, we pass on to them a sense of shame that they may carry all their lives.

On the other hand, when we remain calm, compassionate, and confident, we are more likely to talk with our daughters about their own emotional lives in a creative, appropriate manner.

WHEN FEAR SHOUTS LOUDER THAN LOVE

When the tapes of the past, the troubles of the present, or the terrors of the future direct our mothering, we can't use the natural longing, love, and leading that God has planted in our mother hearts. Furthermore, our emotional state is contagious, and if we want to guide our daughters toward emotional maturity, we must confront our own emotional turmoil and find something stronger and more compelling. The apostle John wrote, "There is no room in love for fear. Well-formed love banishes fear" (1 John 4:18). The next chapter will define well-formed love in the context of mothering and flesh out what it can look like in the real challenges of real life.

For now, the good news is that the mothering we're going to discuss is not about doing everything right, or simply mothering better than our mothers did, or raising perfect Christmas-card children (you know what I mean—those holiday letters describing children who gets straight As, become homecoming queen, and spend every weekend ministering at the nursing home), or ensuring a calm and controlled future. Hand-in-hand mothering is simply a willingness to learn as many ways as you can of responding to your daughter's emotions out of a heart filled with limitless love for her.

Chapter 2

Becoming an Ally—
Using Difficulties
to Build a Relationship

More than what the parents say, the child stores how the parents are in the world.

—Harville Hendrix and Helen Hunt, *Giving the Love That Heals*

The first adolescent client I saw in my counseling practice hurled her Doc Martin shoe through my window. Her parents brought her to see me because she had become moody.

My own children were only eight and nine years old when I began my counseling practice, so when Hillary's mom called to report that her teenage daughter had been withdrawing to her room, was experiencing mood swings, and was yelling at her brother, I smugly thought, *No problem. Bring her to me, and I'll have her smiling and chatting in no time.* After Hillary stared at me stonily for twenty minutes, I felt my own panic begin to mount. *How do you begin a conversation with a sullen statue?*

I began to ask Hillary inane questions and felt like a little yipping poodle dog, begging for any attention she might throw my way. Hillary crossed her legs and started shaking her foot with increasing agitation. My own internal state swirled with growing anxiety. How do you remain calm in the face of a threatening storm?

I resorted to the almost always ineffective counseling question: "Hillary, how do you feel about being here?" Hillary reached for her shoe. I didn't even suspect that her clunky, trendy shoes could become weapons of adolescent angst. Her movements hardly registered with me because I was scrambling to come up with a better question to pierce Hillary's impenetrable shield. How do you get through to a hostile, disinterested teenager?

In a blur of movement Hillary took off her shoe, stood up, and hurled it at my window, shattering the glass. She then picked up her shoe and put it back on her foot. Walking toward the door, Hillary spoke for the first time that hour: "None of this is my fault!" I followed Hillary into the waiting room and looked into her mother's eyes with new compassion. How do you help a moody teenager? I didn't have a clue.

REAL LIFE IS NOT LIKE THE TEXTBOOKS

I knew about adolescent development. I got an A in Adolescent Psychology. But Hillary's visit to my counseling office taught me that theory does not always translate into experience. Of course, my own children have taught me the most. Temper tantrums in the checkout line at the store and emotional meltdowns in the parking lot at church have resulted in both calm and clear thinking on my part *and* my totally losing it. The purpose of this chapter is not to suggest that I have all the answers or that you can parent perfectly. The reality is that all of us, if observed over a long period of parenting, would come out looking both very good and very bad.

My hope is that after reading this chapter and examining your own mothering style, you will be more *intentional* in your mothering—specifically with regard to the emotional development of your daughter. I didn't know it at the time, but when Hillary threw her shoe at my window, I was in a pivotal position to become her ally. Because Hillary's moodiness scared me and her assault on my window shocked me, I missed a significant chance to help her.

In this chapter we are going to examine four mothering styles. These styles are simply *postures* in parenting. Posture is what makes certain activities possible. When I stand, I can walk or run. When I sit, I can lean back and relax. When I kneel, I can pray or scrub the floor. When I lie down, I can rest or sleep. Your posture in response to your daughter's emotions likewise has specific results for both you and your daughter. There is no one right posture in parenting. However, your posture during emotional turbulence determines whether you become your daughter's ally or her sergeant, victim, observer, or even enemy.

For example, my posture with Hillary began as one of superiority. I was going to instruct her into happiness because I was the expert. That posture quickly changed to one of inferiority, as I almost frantically nipped at her heels trying to engage her. In the aftermath of Hillary's shoe launching, my posture changed to that of a victim. And as I surveyed the damage of Hillary's emotional outburst, I felt the distinct possibility of becoming her enemy. I certainly understood why her mother had pushed her into my office, convinced she couldn't handle her own daughter and fearful that no one else could either.

In this chapter you will have a chance to identify your primary posture in mothering and see its strengths and weaknesses. As you become aware of your mothering style, you will have a better chance of quieting your mind, seeing your mistakes, calming your emotions, seeking God's guidance, and creatively guiding your daughter toward emotional maturity. The posture you choose to mother from is significant because it is the perspective from which your daughter will learn to evaluate her own reality, and it is the foundation on which your daughter will build her own emotional life.

As we begin to look at the different mothering styles, remember that good parenting is possible *because* our children struggle, make mistakes, and even melt down completely. The inevitable emotional turbulence of adolescence presents the best context from which to guide our daughters toward emotional maturity. Mary Pipher, in her defining work on adolescent girls, writes: "No girls escape the hurricane. The winds are simply too overpowering."[1]

When a child becomes the focus of negative attention, the mother may experience a complex mix of feelings that are difficult to unravel.... This confusing tangle of emotions blocks the mother from gathering her resources and approaching the problem in a calm, solution-oriented way.

—HARRIET LERNER, *The Mother Dance*

Whether or not you become allies in the storm depends on your perspective. If you see the storm as evidence of your own failure or become angry with your daughter for causing the storm, the chances are good that you and your daughter will become alienated. If you run from the storm or determine to control the gale-force winds, you will miss the chance to bond with your daughter. If you can welcome the storm as an opportunity to forge an alliance with your daughter, you will grow, and your daughter will be on her way to emotional maturity. Pipher concludes with these hopeful words: "When it's storming, it feels like the storm will never end, but the hurricane does end and the sun comes out again."[2]

MOTHERING FROM ABOVE

DAUGHTER: Mom, I hate my life! I don't have any friends. My teachers all hate me, and I just can't face going to school today.

MOM: You don't hate your life. You have lots of friends. Your teachers are there to help you. If you have this kind of attitude, you're not going to be able to learn.

DAUGHTER: But Mom…

MOM: Don't "but" me. Now go get your backpack and get a better attitude. Remember, to have friends, you have to be a friend.

The mom who places herself above her daughter and the emotional turmoil of growing up is most comfortable with teaching, correcting, and instructing. Her response to emotional turbulence is a posture of *talking to* her daughter, which makes dispensing rules and regulations and providing instruction primary. This mom relies on "knowing best" for her daughter.

This mothering style is most effective during our daughters' early years. When our daughters throw temper tantrums in line at Wal-Mart, this is the best posture. Our efforts to understand our daughters' emotional angst and empathize with their feelings will not only prolong their outburst but it may result in disaster. We've all watched harried mothers in the checkout line try the understanding route, only to end up with a shopping cart full of candy and gum bribes and a screaming tyrant holding an entire line of shoppers hostage. Young children need firmness and boundaries, and this mothering style provides the context for consistency and discipline.

The posture of parenting from above works best for teaching behaviors and consequences. When your daughter acts out in the checkout line, she learns that you will calmly pick her up, remove her from the store, and take her home. The storm will pass. As your growing daughter experiences emotional turmoil, this mothering style is less effective. Your daughter learns that you can't remove her distress and that it doesn't evaporate with a smile and a hug from Mom. We moms are sometimes slower to learn that we aren't in control of our daughters' emotional lives.

The mother who insists on parenting from above in the midst of emotional turmoil may have an arsenal of platitudes, but hers will become a voice that falls on deaf ears. For example, the mother in this vignette says some good things: "Teachers are there to help," and "To have friends, you need to be a friend." However, these truths in response to emotional angst fall flat. How do you respond when your friends address your emotional chaos with controlled comments such as "God is good" or "Everything will work out for the best"? Our daughters are no different than we are. When our internal life is swirling around us, we want to know that someone can enter the chaos and be with us.

The mom who places herself above her daughter's emotional turmoil may force the turmoil underground, leaving the daughter alone with her emotions and setting the stage for depression. A growing girl who is constantly lectured or instructed about her emotional life will most often grow to believe her emotions are "bad"—that she has an unruly character that must either be controlled or kept hidden.

Intimacy and high-quality social bonds are seen as the best protection against depression.

—MIRIAM KAUFMAN, *Overcoming Teen Depression*

When our daughters' emotional lives begin to grow and take on many different facets of expression, our primary function is not to force, instruct, or control. In fact, if we parent from this posture, our daughters will quickly conclude that we don't invite and encourage their emotional expression, and they will suspect that it is because there is something wrong with them. Trust in the relationship will wither, and the opportunity for emotional struggle to produce a healthy alliance will be missed.

One indication that you are mothering primarily from above is if you regard your teenage daughter with suspicious contempt. I realize that our teenagers often make choices that erode trust in the parent-child relationship. Compassionate caution is wise, demonstrated by a vigilance on your part that can protect your child while offering her an opportunity to rebuild trust. The destructive suspicion I am referring to is a cynicism about teenagers in general. Common beliefs such as "Teenagers can never be trusted," "Teens are an alien life form," or "Adolescents are nothing but trouble" result in a heart attitude that produces both a sense of superiority on the mother's part and disdain toward the daughter.

No one is ever invited to positive change by being judged. When our goal for our daughters is emotional maturity—an attainment of the heart—our own hearts must be free of contempt and negative judgments. When your daughter embarrasses you in front of the family by her moodiness, do you sincerely want to be her ally in developing emotional maturity, or would you actually like to remain in a position to judge, teach, and be right? When we mother from a posture of being above, it is easy to focus on appearance or form. Changing postures can free us to focus with our daughters on content and substance. For example, the mother in the preceding vignette might simply respond, "That sounds painful and lonely." Her posture changes from *talking to* her daughter to *being with* her.

THE ABOVE MOTHER

Goal: Positive, controlled emotional life.

Role: Instructor, disciplinarian.

Fear: "If I don't dispense rules and wisdom, chaos will reign."

Response to Feelings: "You don't feel that way." "Stop complaining." "Just yesterday you were happy."

Favorite Motherisms: "I know what's best for you." "Happy is as happy does."

Daughter's Response: My emotions are bad and must be suppressed or hidden.

MOTHERING FROM BENEATH

DAUGHTER: Mom, I hate my life! I don't have any friends. My teachers all hate me, and I just can't face going to school today.

MOM: Oh, don't talk like that. I can't stand for you to be so unhappy.

DAUGHTER: But Mom, I can't help it.

MOM: You've got to feel better. I need my happy girl. I'll do anything I
      can to make you happy.

The mother who places herself beneath her daughter sends a strong message: Your emotional life is dangerous, and I can't help you. Furthermore, the mother in this posture may suggest to her daughter that her own emotional well-being is dependent on her daughter's well-being. That's a heavy load for a girl to carry. This posture—in response to a daughter's emotional life— rarely has a positive outcome. A growing daughter needs to know that her mother is stronger than she is and will be her safety net in the world of emotional expression.

This mothering style can be appropriate in the context of admiring our daughters' unique gifts and abilities. I often remind my daughter that she got the athletic ability in our family, and I am amazed at her talents and prowess in sports. I know God has gifted me with different abilities, and that confidence frees me to admire my daughter. But when it comes to emotional expression, placing ourselves beneath our daughters results in disconnection and another missed opportunity to become our daughters' allies.

In this vignette, it could be appropriate for the mother to mirror back to her daughter the magnitude of the emotion: "You sound very unhappy." But as we mirror our daughters' emotions, we must also reflect our own clarity and calmness: "I want to hear more about what's going on at school. Let's go to Starbucks after school today and talk about your life."

The good news is that we don't need to have the capacity to solve all our daughters' problems, but we do need to convey the message "I'm with you." While we are communicating our compassionate attention, our posture needs to assure our daughters that *we* are okay, that our own emotional climate is not regulated by their thermostats.

THE BENEATH MOTHER

Goal: Have her own emotional needs met by her daughter's emotional
       stability.

Role: Victim of daughter's emotional life.

Fear: "If my daughter's not happy, I can't be happy." "I don't have what it takes to help my daughter."

Response to Feelings: Panic, powerlessness.

Favorite Motherism: "That's my happy girl."

Daughter's Response: Feels pressure to be happy and to hide anything negative because she feels responsible for her mother's well-being.

Mothering from a Distance

DAUGHTER: Mom, I hate my life! I don't have any friends. My teachers all hate me, and I just can't face going to school today.

MOM: Come on now, you need to get ready for school.

DAUGHTER: But Mom, didn't you hear me?

MOM: I heard you, but we can't be late. Let's get going.

The mother who places herself at a distance from her daughter is in a posture to dispassionately observe or simply disengage from her daughter's life. Knowing when to step in or step out is a skill that is developed as a mother knows her daughter, knows her own strengths and weaknesses, and knows which combinations result in emotional growth.

Allowing our daughters to learn from their own mistakes and develop confidence in their growing abilities is an essential component of emotional maturity. However, if we are distant from our daughters for any reason other than to promote their growth and development, our daughters may perceive that this distance means that something is wrong with them, and they may conclude that they can count only on themselves during the storms of life.

When our daughters begin to experience mood swings and the roller coaster of emotions that come with adolescence, they need us. They need us to tell them they're normal and that they can express themselves and be safe and supported along the way. Our posture in the midst of their emotional turbulence not only can make positive self-regard and self-image possible, but it can also provide the foundation for what our daughters will believe about relationships. The conclusion that I am alone in this world and must rely only on myself is a lonely and exhausting approach to life. When we distance ourselves from our daughters' emotional expressions, we may launch them on a lifelong course of resigned self-reliance.

The mother in the preceding vignette might signal to her daughter that the emotional angst needs to be put on "hold" so that they can each perform the necessary tasks of the day, but she can send this signal with a promise for reconnection: "I know you're feeling awful and it will be hard to get through this day. I promise I will pray for you today. Let's make a date to sit in front of the fireplace tonight, drink hot chocolate, and talk."

When we enter our daughters' emotional worlds with acceptance and interest, we send the message that supports the Irish proverb, "In the shelter of each other we were meant to live."

THE DISTANT MOTHER

Goal: Provide basic needs for her daughter.

Role: Observer.

Fear: "If I get involved, I will make things worse or get sucked into the chaos."

Response to Feelings: No comment.

Favorite Motherism: "Grow up." "Get over it."

Daughter's Response: I am on my own.

MOTHERING FROM TOO CLOSE

DAUGHTER: Mom, I hate my life! I don't have any friends. My teachers all hate me, and I just can't face going to school today.

MOM: Oh, honey. You have lots of friends. Why don't we call Melissa and Amber and see if they can come over this weekend?

DAUGHTER: Mom, we're not friends anymore. They don't like me. I don't want to be with them. I just need to stay home from school today.

MOM: I know they like you. Why don't I call their mothers? You can stay home, and I know you'll feel better tomorrow. I'll call your teachers and go by the school and pick up all your homework so you won't get behind.

The mom who mothers from too close is the "hover mother" who wants everyone to be happy and content. A mother who takes this posture in response to her daughter's emotional turmoil will feel frustrated and frantic. If Mary Pipher's description of normal female adolescence is true, the hover mother is in for a bumpy ride.

> Something dramatic happens to girls in early adolescence. Just as planes
> and ships disappear mysteriously into the Bermuda Triangle, so do
> the selves of girls go down in droves.… Girls become fragmented,
> their selves split into mysterious contradictions. They are sensitive and
> tenderhearted, mean and competitive, superficial and idealistic. They
> are confident in the morning and overwhelmed with anxiety by night-
> fall. They rush through their days with wild energy and then collapse in
> lethargy.[3]

Moms who believe they can and should keep up with every change, solve every problem, and soothe every hurt will either be mad at their daughters for being so complicated or will condemn themselves for continually falling short.

When a hover mother responds to her daughter's emotional turmoil with a determination to "fix" it, she sends the message that emotions are something to be fixed rather than clues to be followed. The hover mother also suggests to her daughter that she cannot help herself. While the mom who mothers from a distance teaches her daughter that she must rely on herself alone, the mom who mothers from too close sends the message that her daughter can't rely on herself at all. Suppressing all pain and discomfort eliminates a necessary context in which her daughter can grow and find her own internal resources for handling difficulties.

The mother in this vignette might still offer to be active in her daughter's life while she affirms her daughter's emotional reality: "I am so sorry you are having a rough day. Is there anything you would like from me that might help?"

THE HOVER MOTHER
Goal: A happy daughter.
Role: Cheerleader, caretaker.

Fear: "I am responsible for everything that happens to my daughter, and if I can't make her happy, I am not a good mother."

Response to Feelings: "What can I do to fix things and make you happy?"

Favorite Motherism: "Let mom kiss it and make it all better."

Daughter's Response: She may withdraw from the smothering with a mean-spiritedness or become self-absorbed with a spirit of entitlement and little thought of others.

JUST FOR YOU

Your answers to the following questions will help you further identify your primary mothering style. Remember that the goal of this exercise is not to find out everything you're doing "wrong," but to discover your primary posture in mothering.

1. When my daughter is angry, I:
   a. lecture/punish ✓
   b. feel anxious
   c. walk away
   d. become a cheerleader
2. When my daughter is sad, I:
   a. lecture/punish
   b. feel afraid ✓
   c. walk away
   d. become tearful
3. When my daughter is happy, I:
   a. feel successful
   b. feel happy ✓
   c. feel distant
   d. feel responsible
4. When my daughter is moody, I:
   a. lecture/punish
   b. feel moody ✓

    c.   am disgusted

    d.   feel responsible

5. When my daughter feels lonely and as if she doesn't belong, I:

    a.   tell her to call a friend

    b.   try to be her friend

    c.   tell her everyone feels that way ✓

    d.   feel responsible

6. When my daughter withdraws from the family, I:

    a.   punish her and make her join the family

    b.   feel as if I've done something wrong

    c.   let her be by herself ✓

    d.   try to get everyone to include her

7. When my daughter won't talk about her feelings, I:

    a.   scold her

    b.   am intimidated by her silence

    c.   leave her alone ✓

    d.   try to articulate her feelings for her

8. When my daughter is rude to others, I:

    a.   punish her

    b.   feel embarrassed

    c.   ignore her ✓

    d.   apologize for her

9. When my daughter is giddy and silly, I:

    a.   tell her to calm down ✓

    b.   feel embarrassed

    c.   ignore her

    d.   try to keep her happy

10. When my daughter fights with her brother or sister, I:

    a.   lecture/punish

    b.   take sides

    c.   walk away

    d.   try to keep the peace ✓

(continued on the following page)

11. When my daughter does not do well in school/activities, I:

    a.   lecture/punish/structure new rules

    b.   feel like a bad mother

    c.   let her work it out

    d.   start doing her work for her

12. When my daughter succeeds in school/activities, I:

    a.   feel successful

    b.   feel like a good mother

    c.   don't say much

    d.   feel responsible

If most of your answers were "a," your mothering style is from above. If most of your answers were "b," your mothering style is from beneath. If you mostly answered "c," your mothering style is from a distance. If most of your answers were "d," you tend to be a hover mother.

ENOUGH GUILT FOR NOW, THANK YOU

Identifying your mothering style may be the easy part. Not feeling guilty is the hard part. As you become aware of your posture in mothering, you may feel guilty about lecturing or feel guilty because you didn't know what to say. You may feel guilty about not being involved or feel guilty because you were too involved. No doubt you will feel guilty about feeling guilty.

Of course, guilt is not all bad. Just as pain in the body may be a warning of physical injury or sickness, guilt may be an ache in the soul that prompts us to examine our motives and behaviors. I hope any guilt you are feeling after reading this chapter will motivate you to identify your mothering style and determine whether it connects you with your daughter in her emotional development or disconnects you from her. If you recognize disconnecting behaviors in your mothering style, let go of guilt, and think and pray about trying a different posture.

Perhaps your guilt will be assuaged if you remember that the challenges we are discussing—the emotional turbulence of adolescence and your response to it—provide the perfect context in which to form a powerful alliance with your daughter. In the next chapter we will look in detail at the emotional development of girls and discover ways to respond calmly, compassionately, and creatively.

Whenever emotional turmoil threatens, I remember my first counseling session with Hillary, and calmly suggest that everyone take off their shoes!

Being a Teenage Girl Is Not Easy

Any 4-year-old who likes ladybugs and lightning bolts can tell you that life is wildly beautiful as far as the eye can see. But it took the geniuses of our time to reveal how beautifully ordered life is deep down where we can't see it all—in the molecular workshop where we become who we are.

—JAMES WATSON, "The Secret of Life," *Time* Magazine, February 2003

Growing up female is not easy. When you combine the chemical and hormonal changes that are a natural part of female development with the cultural pressures and challenges facing adolescent girls, it's a wonder that girls don't lose their minds completely—and that their mothers don't too! Living with an adolescent girl provides lots of evidence against the "beautifully ordered life" described by scientist James Watson in the quotation above. Unless you think tornadoes, hurricanes, and roller coasters are examples of beautiful order.

Understanding female emotional development, knowing your daughter, and believing heart and soul that there are a few unshakable truths you can cling to during the storms of emotional development can make the process more intentional and meaningful. You can use this information to inform your mothering and infuse it with purpose for your daughter, and that in turn will have a profound effect on your daughter's emotional growth.

Have you ever looked at one of those pictures that appears to be a jumble of squiggles and colors, but actually contains a hidden three-dimensional design? Sometimes if you focus your eyes just the right way, you can spot the intended image. Sometimes you need someone else to tell you what you're looking for. In this chapter we will focus on what you can look for in the midst of your daughter's emotional turmoil that will connect the two of you in the same pursuit: your daughter's emotional maturity.

UNDERSTANDING YOUR DAUGHTER'S BIOLOGY

As soon as we got into the car to go to the grocery store yesterday, Kristin lamented, "I feel so stressed out. I can't figure out why, but I feel like I'm about to explode!"

I replied with a question that Kristin knows is always my first line of defense in the midst of emotional turbulence: "Could it be hormones?"

I loved (and identified with) Kristin's answer. "Of course it could be hormones, Mom. It's always hormones. I calculate that I get about two good days a month that aren't messed up by hormones!"

We dissolved into laughter, but only because we both understood exactly what Kristin was talking about. Doesn't every woman? Still, that doesn't mean we fully understand our own biology. Understanding female biology and its unique impact on the emotional life is a gift that will help you and your daughter demystify some of what is going on.

Oh yes, you shaped me first inside, then out;
you formed me in my mother's womb.
I thank you,...God—you're breathtaking!
Body and soul, I am marvelously made!

—PSALM 139:13,14

At the onset of puberty (which can occur anytime between the ages of eight and fourteen), a girl's body is flooded with hormones. These hormones not only cause physical changes but also result in the increasingly unstable mix of feelings that girls experience. Your daughter may tell you that she doesn't feel like herself anymore, and for good reason. She is changing, and part of a mother's job is to help her daughter recognize and welcome the changes.

Perhaps one of the biggest changes that a young girl goes through in the transition of adolescence is the new experience of intense moods and emotions. The female brain starts to respond more intensely to emotion. Feelings, especially sadness, trigger neurons in an area *eight times larger* in the female brain than in the male brain.[1] That explains some things, doesn't it? All of a sudden your daughter becomes aware of a wide range of feelings over which she seems to have no control. A lot of this fluctuation of mood is due to hormones.

Just for the Two of You

This is a good time to make sure you and your daughter have had meaningful and informed conversations about menstruation and the various biological changes that occur during adolescence. Helpful resources are listed in the resources section on page 209 under the heading "Female Development."

Buy a fun calendar just for the purpose of charting the hormonal cycle. Rate each day on a scale of 1 to 10, where 1 describes a day your daughter feels really crummy and 10 describes a day when she feels great. Notice the patterns. If there are regular patterns, you can help your daughter predict and prepare for moody times related to her monthly cycle.

Help your daughter make sense of her hormones. It may be that on the days before her period, she will feel more energetic and confident, or she may feel the most miserable. You can encourage her to take advantage of this time by tackling certain projects or activities or being especially kind to herself.

During her period, she may feel more reflective and quiet, especially if she experiences physical discomfort or cramps. You can encourage her to pamper herself, listen to music or write in her journal, and take Aleve! In the days following her period, she may feel a growing restlessness. This is a good time to encourage your daughter to set new goals and make plans for the days ahead.

If the patterns are erratic (and they often are for young girls at the beginning of puberty), you can assure your daughter that her mood swings reflect her hormonal instability and that she can hang on until her hormones level out.

MOODINESS, MARSHMALLOWS, AND MEMORY

I learned an important principle for mothering in the midst of moodiness from a 1960s Stanford University study about four-year-olds and marshmallows. The researcher called the children one by one into a room and offered each a marshmallow. He told the child that he or she could eat the marshmallow immediately or wait for him to come back from an errand, and then he would give the child two marshmallows. Some of the children waited, distracting themselves by resting their heads on their arms, fidgeting, or talking to themselves. About one-third of the group ate the marshmallow as soon as the man left.

What is remarkable about this test is its diagnostic power. Twelve years later the same children were tracked down as adolescents and tested again. Researcher Daniel Goleman describes the children who delayed gratification and resisted the marshmallow: "They were less likely to go to pieces, freeze or regress under stress, or become rattled and disorganized when pressured; they embraced challenges and pursued them instead of giving up even in the face of difficulties; they were self-reliant and confident, trustworthy and dependable." The children who had grabbed the marshmallow were "more likely to be seen as shying away from social contacts, to be stubborn and indecisive, to be easily upset by frustrations, to think of themselves as 'bad' or unworthy, to regress or become immobilized by stress,...to overreact to irritations with a sharp temper."[2]

To change [a negative view], we actually have to change the brain chemistry by remembering positive things.

—DANIEL G. AMEN, *Change Your Brain, Change Your Life*

All because of a lone marshmallow? Goleman explains that it has to do with brain chemistry. If emotional memories involving temper, frustration, anxiety, depression, and moodiness pile up in early adolescence, brain chemicals will hijack the rest of the brain by flooding it with strong and inappropriate emotions. But if the emotions stored are those of restraint, self-awareness, self-regulation, hope, and optimism, our daughters become endowed with an "emotional intelligence" that serves rather than enslaves them for the rest of their lives.

The good news is that the brain is ever changing and is impacted by our choices and behaviors. Emotional intelligence can be taught as we help our daughters identify and monitor the emotional turmoil of adolescence. If emotional storms in adolescence are inevitable, our daughters need to know just as surely that they can and will weather the storms. Their memories of past storms and how they survived will give them faith and hope for the future. We can remind our daughters of biological realities that will calm and com-

JUST FOR THE TWO OF YOU

Mothers are the keepers of memory. Keep a journal that records not only your daughter's activities, but her emotional development as well. Note when she is kind, adventurous, giving, and self-reliant. Read and reread the journal together. When the going gets rough and your daughter loses sight of who she is, remind her with the evidence you have compiled.

Create times of remembrance. Recall happy, sweet, fun, meaningful times. Describe them to one another in detail, using as many of the five senses as possible. What colors do you remember? What smells? Is the memory connected to music? If your daughter is in the midst of a particularly moody, unpleasant season in life, it is easy for both of you to focus on the negative. It is natural when your daughter is rebellious, sullen, and withdrawn to focus only on the negative experiences. It seems crazy to remember the good times in the midst of a hurricane. Remembering, however, not only changes brain chemistry but can draw you and your daughter together to a place of calm in the midst of the storm.

Plan responses that will jog her memory and remind her that this turmoil will pass. These sentences are not for the purpose of dismissing your daughter's feelings or trivializing your response. But in the midst of an emotional flareup, it's easy to forget the truth and respond in anger or hurt. Tell your daughter that these responses are not the end of the conversation but a bridge to future conversation and a protection against fueling the fire. Your daughter may roll her eyes, laugh at you, or even get mad, but she will also feel a growing confidence that her capricious emotions are not in control of you.

fort them during the hormonal fluctuations of being female. We can also remind our daughters of their past resilience, self-control, or simply survival during prior emotional angst, and those memories will actually build "muscles" in the brain for the emotional work of the future.

Amy came to see me when she was a sophomore in high school. Her freshman year had been disastrous. She felt like she didn't fit in; she didn't make many friends, and she dissolved into tears every day after school. She

Here are a few ideas to get you started with new responses:

Instead of: You never listen to me.

Try: I get frustrated when you don't listen to me, but I know you have listened and will listen again.

Instead of: Things aren't that bad.

Try: I know things seem hard right now. (Note the urge to add something to this sentence. Sometimes we need to just let our daughters feel what they are feeling.)

Instead of: You need to stop blaming everyone else and take responsibility.

Try: It seems like you're not the only one going through a hard time. Your friends (teachers, etc.) are too. What can you do to make the situation better, even if it doesn't change?

Instead of: You are not fat (ugly, stupid, etc.).

Try: You are not fat. You are so pretty. I love your thick, wavy hair. You are not ugly. Remember how great you felt in that outfit you wore to school last Thursday? You are not stupid. You have a great sense of other people's feelings. Remember when you knew your friend was upset even before she told anyone?

hated her life. After a few hours together, I learned that Amy loved music. She was in her high-school choir, and it was the highlight of her day. I asked her to take specific note of how she felt during this hour of school. She reported that she felt like she belonged, she felt she was good at something, and she felt moments of joy in singing the music. I asked Amy to experiment with focusing on these positive memories during the harder moments of her day.

Amy explained how this worked for her. She walked into the school lunchroom and felt overwhelmed with negative emotions. She said she sat down and took a few deep breaths and then reminded herself that she would be going to choir in an hour. She explained to me, "I told myself, 'Relax. Lunch will be over soon. Everyone is not looking at you and thinking that you're a freak. You will go to choir and sing something amazing, and you will feel good.'"

JUST FOR YOU

Your mothering style will influence how you guide your daughter toward emotional maturity. Following are a few hints for each mothering style.

1. *From above.* You will be tempted to tell your daughter that she is under the influence of hormones, and your daughter may react to these biology lessons by resisting self-awareness. When your daughter connects her moods to her hormonal cycle, affirm her self-discovery. Let her feel that she is teaching you.

2. *From below.* Don't fall into the trap of commiserating with your daughter about being victims of your biology. You can empathize about mood swings and monthly physical discomfort, but do so by affirming that being female is a gift that comes with intuition, relational skills, and the fun of nail polish and lipstick!

3. *From a distance.* Don't shortchange yourself or your daughter by merely observing her biological and emotional changes. One sure way to connect with your daughter in the midst of these changes is by sharing your own experience of female development.

4. *From too close.* Remember, your role is not to make the moodiness go away, but to guide your daughter in experiences that confirm to her that she has a growing number of resources to rely on in the midst of emotional turmoil.

Amy's sophomore year is almost over, and she's not any more excited about school than she was at the beginning of the year. She doesn't expect her high-school world to suddenly become a warm and fuzzy place, but she does trust herself more in the midst of this world. Amy's self-confidence has grown, and her internal work has assured her that bad feelings will come and go.

One of the most important responses in mothering during emotional turmoil is, "I know you feel bad right now. You will not always feel this way." It is easy for both mothers and daughters to become enveloped in the mood of the moment. As we remember that emotions come and go, we have faith in the possibilities of the future.

KNOWING YOUR DAUGHTER'S BIOGRAPHY

Your daughter's emotional climate is not just controlled by biology; it is also influenced by biography—her story. Her accumulated experiences tell who she is. When a girl reaches adolescence, much of the work of growing up takes place out of the parents' sight. Adolescent psychologists suggest that for an average child, only about 10 percent of her emotional ups and downs are a result of family issues. Reed Larson, Professor of Human Development at the University of Illinois, suggests that the "majority of adolescents' emotions are caused by peer relations.... Emotions often go up and down over someone they haven't even talked to. By the high school years, romantic relationships [or their absence] account for over one-third of positive and negative extreme emotions in adolescents."[3] This probably comes as both good and bad news. We mothers can breathe a sigh of relief—*It's not my fault!*—only to feel increasing anxiety—*It's out of my control!*

But the people...grumbled against Moses.... Then the LORD said to Moses, "Write this on a scroll as something to be remembered...."

—EXODUS 17:3,14, NIV

Statistics and stories confirm that the world our girls are growing up in is often a cold, cruel place. Bullying, sexual harassment, and profane utterances are daily realities in teenage life. Boys don't just call girls "fat" or "ugly" anymore; they mimic the words of their musical icons and label girls "bitch" and "slut." Girls aren't much nicer to one another. Research from the 1990s suggests that an incident of bullying takes places once every seven minutes in school[4] and that by the eighth grade, 81 percent of girls have experienced sexual harassment.[5] When you add these startling statistics to more familiar stories of gossip, breakups, and jealousy, you have a relational climate that easily explains our daughters' tumultuous emotional climate.

JUST FOR THE TWO OF YOU

1. *Feelings are essential to being human.* Without our feelings, we become like robots without distinction or passion. Feelings make the story interesting. Try watching a movie with your daughter. Note together how boring or one-dimensional the story would be without emotions. Our feelings actually express the highest ideals of our complex brain: courage, loyalty, love, and so on.

2. *Feelings are not always crazy or irrational.* Often our emotions are perfectly rational and are a natural consequence of our experiences. Even when feelings seem irrational, they may be rooted in biological realities. It is a gift to say to your daughter, "It makes sense that you are feeling that way." It is a way of validating her story.

3. *Feelings serve a purpose.* Every emotion has a cause and a purpose. For example, anger is usually caused by something or someone violating our boundaries, and its purpose is to mobilize us to protect ourselves and those we love. Fear can be caused when our intuition senses that we are in danger, and its purpose is to lead us to safety. Tell your daughter about a time your intuition and the accompanying emotion of fear or uneasiness served you. I love one of my grandmother's stories about raising a family during the Dust Bowl days. She had a hunch that she needed to go pick up my father out of his crib. As soon as she held him, a ferocious dust storm swept through the house, causing the roof to collapse on top of his crib. Not only does my grandmother's story fascinate me with details of another time and part of my family history, but it also encourages me to pay attention to my thoughts and feelings about my daughter.

THE POWER OF EMOTION

The good news begins by returning to biological realities. During puberty, our daughters have the capacity to become much more sensitive to feelings, hunches, and all of the subtleties going on around them. We have the opportunity to teach our daughters that their emotions are a personal radar system telling them what they need in life, what they should stay away from, and how they can connect with others. In the chapters to come, we will address lots of ways you can connect with your daughter in the midst of her challenging world. We will also examine things you can do together to hone your daughter's relational skills in the midst of her own emotional development.

Right now it is important to lay a foundation between you and your

JUST FOR YOU

It's easy to go on autopilot and allow your mothering style to dictate how you respond to your daughter's emotions. Following are a few reminders that will guide you in responding to your daughter's emotions with intentionality and wisdom.

1. *From above.* Remember this is your daughter's story. Resist the impulse to require your daughter to feel as you would feel.

2. *From beneath.* When you feel overwhelmed by your daughter's emotions, take a few seconds to pray and turn her over to the care of God. She doesn't need you to take the feelings away, but instead to offer your presence.

3. *From a distance.* When your daughter expresses an emotion, be curious. Ask her, "What happened that made you feel like this?" Your curiosity will increase your daughter's self-awareness while it connects the two of you.

4. *From too close.* When bad behavior and emotional expression go hand in hand, allow the resulting consequences. If your daughter's friends or siblings (or you) are hurt or angry because of her emotional outburst, don't minimize the impact. You might say, "I know you were hurting, but your words hurt others as well."

daughter for dealing with the inevitable changing emotions that will come as her story unfolds. What *you* feel about feelings will determine whether you become allies, moving together toward emotional maturity, or whether your daughter will hide from you because she suspects that you fear or dislike her emerging emotional life. What you feel about feelings can also give your daughter hope about who she is becoming in the tumultuous process of growing up.

INVITING YOUR DAUGHTER TO BE THE BELOVED

The goal of emotional expression is not just the venting of everything we feel. If we were primitive animals, we could freely give in to all our emotions and live them out with no restraint. But that is not the final purpose of our emotions. Our emotions were ultimately designed by God to enable us to love. Without feelings we could not connect meaningfully to another person or to God. As you prepare to guide your daughter toward emotional maturity, every road leads to love—inviting your daughter to receive and give love. You will be able to do this only to the degree that you know you yourself are beloved.

Someone once asked the great contemplative Thomas Merton, "Who are you?" His answer: "I am the one beloved by God." Is there something that keeps you from answering as Merton did? Failure? Success? Disappointment? Confusing emotions?

The brain is a good stagehand. It gets on with its work while we're busy acting out our scenes. When we see an object, the whole peninsula of our senses wakes up to appraise the new sight. All the brain's shopkeepers consider it from their point of view.

—DIANE ACKERMAN, *A Natural History of the Senses*

Your design—your biology as well as your biography—comes from the hands of a Designer who is madly in love with you. Who longs for a relationship with you more than anything else. Who is committed to a relationship with you above everything else. Whose entire story is about His design for a relationship with you. God designed you for a relationship with Him. This is

JUST FOR YOU

Our view of God is important because it influences how we *are* in the world. Meditating on the following passages from Scripture can deeply impact your view of God and how it translates to your mothering style:

1. *From above.* God's love is not contingent on what you do. "Answer this question: Does the God who lavishly provides you with his own presence, his Holy Spirit, working things in your lives you could never do for yourselves, does he do these things because of your strenuous moral striving or because you trust him to do them in you? Don't these things happen among you just as they happened with Abraham? He believed God, and that act of belief was turned into a life that was right with God" (Galatians 3:5-6).

2. *From beneath.* Any sense of personal unworthiness on our part does not limit God's love. His love makes us worthy. "Do you think anyone is going to be able to drive a wedge between us and Christ's love for us? There is no way! Not trouble, not hard times, not hatred, not hunger, not homelessness, not bullying threats, not backstabbing, not even the worst sins listed in Scripture" (Romans 8:35).

3. *From a distance.* God is not unmoved or removed from us. "Before I was born the LORD called me; from my birth he has made mention of my name.... Can a mother forget the baby at her breast and have no compassion on the child she has borne? Though she may forget, I will not forget you! See, I have engraved you on the palms of my hands" (Isaiah 49:1,15-16, NIV).

4. *From too close.* God longs for a real relationship with us, but not merely as a vending machine to give us what we want. We short-change our relationship with our children when we succumb to merely indulging them and not believing that the difficulties of life deepen relationship. "'With everlasting kindness I will have compassion on you,' says the LORD your Redeemer.... 'Though the mountains be shaken and the hills be removed, yet my unfailing love for you will not be shaken nor my covenant of peace be removed'" (Isaiah 54:8,10, NIV).

the original purpose of each human life. Being beloved is our identity, the core of our existence. It is not merely a lofty thought, an inspiring idea, or one name among many. It is the name by which God knows us, the way He relates to us, and the model for our mothering.

How does God respond to you when you throw a temper tantrum or are grouchy, ungrateful, sad, or happy? As you consider walking hand in hand with your daughter through the turmoil of adolescence, you are in for a bumpy ride. To the degree that you know you are beloved, however, you will be able to invite your daughter into that same reality.

Mothering is at its best when we are in the circle of receiving and giving love and inviting our daughters to the same. What a high and holy calling!

We can increase our daughters' faith in the possibilities of the present as we understand their biology. We can fuel our daughters' hope for the future as we invite and creatively respond to their emotional expressions in the midst of their unfolding biographies. And we can model for our daughters the life of love as we are firmly rooted in the unshakable truth that God loves us. Experiencing God's love in the midst of the turbulence of our daughters' adolescence is the most important mothering matter.

> We don't yet see things clearly. We're squinting in a fog, peering
> through a mist. But it won't be long before the weather clears and the
> sun shines bright! We'll see it all then, see it all as clearly as God sees us,
> knowing him directly just as he knows us!
>
> But for right now, until that completeness, we have three things to
> do to lead us toward that consummation: Trust steadily in God, hope
> unswervingly, love extravagantly. And the best of the three is love.
> (1 Corinthians 13:12,13)

Becoming an Ally—Moving Toward Emotional Maturity

*Now, I'm forty-six, and the mother of three teenagers, two of whom are
girls. As I struggle with hot flashes, insomnia, mood swings, and efforts to
control my weight, my daughters are battling with PMS and trying to figure out who they are and where in the world they fit in. All three of us are
in the midst of major hormonal upheavals, and each of us thinks that her
predicament is worse than the other's.*

—DIANA MARQUISE RAAB, quoted in *Surviving Ophelia*

The telephone rang at 5:30 a.m. My neighbor was waiting for the early
morning call. Her daughter, a member of the Army Reserve, had
recently been deployed and had promised that she would call when she had
some news about her next destination.

Cheryl was now seated at my kitchen table trying to recall every detail of
the early morning connection with her daughter. Cheryl's hands trembled as
she picked up her cup of coffee. "She said she was in Spain and that in less
than four hours they would be on a ship headed for the Middle East." Tears
started to trickle down Cheryl's face.

"She told me that she was scared and asked me to pray for her." Fear
flickered in Cheryl's eyes, and then she began to weep. "I started to tell her
that I'd pray…and then we lost connection…that was it…she was gone."

Cheryl and I sat at my kitchen table for a long time, and we cried
together for all the men and women caught in the complicated conflict in the
Middle East. We also cried for the mother and daughter caught in the agonizing, profoundly simple loss of one another. Of course, Cheryl and her

daughter remained connected by love and prayers, and yet the connection broken by space and time could not be denied.

I could not help but think of the countless mothers and daughters who sit in my counseling office, not separated by time and space as Cheryl and her daughter were but just as surely disconnected and often in the midst of similarly frightening and chaotic turmoil. Sometimes mothers blame their daughters for the disconnection and point to a culture that encourages distance and even disrespect for parents. Sometimes daughters blame their mothers for the disconnection and begin to list all the ways their parents "just don't understand."

The loss of the daughter to the mother, the mother to the daughter,
is the essential female tragedy.

—ADRIENNE RICH, *Of Women Born*

One thing is certain, whether it is mothers complaining about daughters or daughters about mothers, the importance of the connection and the disruption that occurs as a result of disconnection are undeniable.

I will never forget the time this realization dawned on one of my moody adolescent clients. Jackie was eloquent in describing her mother's failures. "She just totally doesn't get it, and she makes me so mad I want to scream," Jackie concluded her diatribe against her mother.

Much to Jackie's and her mother's surprise, I replied: "Wow, your mom is really important to you."

They both looked at me as though I was the one who totally didn't get it.

"I don't think you would spend so much time thinking and talking about your mother's failures if you didn't feel like the connection between you and your mom—good or bad—is significant," I explained. "Your complaints reveal that you want something different. And given that your complaints are primarily about your mother, I would guess that what you are wanting and needing most right now is something from your mother."

Jackie looked at me with a mixture of cynicism and hope in her eyes. "You mean *my mom* is the answer to what I'm looking for?"

Jackie wasn't convinced that I was right. And neither was her mother. In the midst of turmoil, we look for someone to take the blame, and that someone for many a teenage girl is her mother. When hormones are fluctuating, peers are unpredictable, and emotions get dragged along for a bumpy ride, teenage girls often make sense of their nonsensical world by turning to their moms and exclaiming, "It's all *your* fault."

When we as moms get pulled into our daughters' quicksand of blame and confusion, we cannot be allies to help them toward emotional maturity. We become as paralyzed in the sludge of emotional turmoil as our daughters are.

YOUR DAUGHTER IS NOT YOUR ENEMY

It may seem like the answer lies in pointing our fingers at our moody, combative (or withdrawn) daughters and exclaiming, "No, it's all *your* fault." But it's impossible to connect with someone who we believe is our enemy. Even though your daughter may be moody, sullen, angry, or withdrawn, *she is not your enemy.* Any thought that relegates your daughter to that position is destructive to the relationship and is a roadblock to making positive change. This is where it can get a little tricky, but this is where the heart of hand-in-hand mothering is developed.

- Is your daughter prickly and hard to love right now? Remember, *you are not at war with your daughter.*
- Does your daughter fluctuate from one mood to another, leaving you to decipher her unexplained emotions? Remember, *you are not at war with your daughter.*
- Does your daughter become secretive at times about her feelings and retreat to her room, the telephone, or the Internet to commiserate with friends, shutting you out? Remember, *you are not at war with your daughter.*
- Does your daughter yell, slam doors, hurl insults, and leave carnage from her emotional volatility all through the house? Remember, *you are not at war with your daughter.*

But you are at war. You are at war *for* the emotional maturity of your daughter. This war requires that you remain rooted in your love for and your commitment to your daughter and your belief in your unique gifts and abilities to mother her. This is a war that requires empathy for your daughter's emotional experiences and appreciation for what she brings to the relationship. This is a war that requires the determination to find every way of connection possible and to steer clear of communication that might result in disconnection.

In this chapter we are going to identify the "seven deadly sins" of mothering that result in disconnection and defeat your attempts to become your daughter's ally in moving toward emotional maturity. Allowing these "sins" to become habitual in your mothering will damage the relationship and keep you from helping your daughter during these difficult days.

In contrast, we will then examine the "seven essential skills" of mothering, which are habits that connect you with your daughter. When you develop these habits, you can approach the emotional turmoil of adolescence with your daughter in the same spirit as two explorers might approach an adventure: You can share maps, support each other in the venture, and anticipate together the difficult challenges and amazing vistas you will see!

DENYING VS. ASKING QUESTIONS

Jackie and her mother came back for their second visit. They looked at each other warily. I asked Jackie, "So, what have you thought about since last week when we talked about the significance of your relationship with your mother?"

"Well," Jackie began, "I just don't think she gets it. My life is so hard right now, and I don't really see what the point of it all is. I mean, so you go to school, and then what? You have to go to college, and then you have to get a job, and then you have to get married and have a family and all of the problems that go with that. And I don't even know if I believe in God. I mean if He is so smart and everything, why did He make life so that it's just one problem after another?"

Before Jackie could finish, her mother cut into the conversation. "Oh, Jackie, you don't mean that. You have always believed in God ever since you were a little girl."

That was it. Disconnection. The well-meaning interruption of Jackie's mom denied Jackie's feelings and disconnected the conversation. When a mom denies her daughter's feelings or thoughts, she acts as if she wants to erase her daughter's inner experiences, which feels like rejection to the daughter.

Fear is usually the culprit when denial becomes a pattern in mothering. We're afraid of our daughters' doubts, anger, or sadness and respond by saying, "You don't feel the way you're feeling." We have spent our daughters' entire lives protecting them from harm, and it feels counterintuitive to allow negative emotions into the conversation. We're afraid that the negative feelings will stay or steer our daughters toward harmful behaviors.

If teens do not feel accepted at home, rejection from even one or two of their peers is magnified a hundredfold.

—PATRICIA EVANS, *Teen Torment*

Allowing our daughters to express negative emotions as well as doubts and fears is essential for their emotional development. Rationally, we know that whether or not we "let" them express these emotions, our daughters are going to experience anger, confusion, and sadness. The question is whether they are going to experience these emotions in the context of their relationship *with us*—or not.

When we try to keep our daughters from experiencing a particular emotion, we run the risk that they will hide the emotion from us and seek input from other sources that may be questionable or unreliable. When a feeling goes unexpressed, the thoughts behind the feeling continue to operate, but

JUST FOR YOU

The art of asking questions is developed just as surely as any other skill or creative expression. Listed below are some negative emotions and a question that might open the door to further connection with your daughter. Add to the list your own questions that you can ask when your daughter is in the midst of emotional angst.

Anger: What are you most angry about?

Sadness: What hurts the most in this situation?

Doubt: What other questions does this make you want to ask?

Fear: What feels out of your control right now?

Jealousy: What are you afraid will be taken away from you in this situation?

with far more power than before. When we can quiet our fears and ask our daughters questions about what they are feeling, we become their allies.

Your curiosity about what is underneath your daughter's emotions and expressions teaches her to use her feelings and preferences to grow in emotional maturity. In Jackie's case, her mom might have listened to her daughter finish her thoughts, and then said, "Oh, Jackie! I had no idea you were feeling this way. When did you start feeling like life is so pointless?" She could express empathy, admit her own ignorance about her daughter's inner world, and ask a question that might start to draw out the reason for Jackie's despair.

IGNORING VS. LISTENING

"I think I must interrupt Jackie all the time," her mom admitted.

Jackie jumped right in at her mother's first admission of failure. "You don't just interrupt. You act like you don't even hear me half the time."

Teenagers are good at sniffing out what they perceive as weakness and trying to use it to their advantage, especially if they are feeling hurt and powerless themselves.

Jackie's mother responded with such humility and wisdom, I knew that this mother and daughter were going to have a great relationship with a little coaching. "I'm really not surprised you feel that way," she said. "I think I act like I'm not listening when I'm not sure what to say, afraid of your emotions, or trying to keep a fight from breaking out."

Her lack of defensiveness disarmed Jackie's attack, and they both looked to me for direction as to where to go next.

Ignoring their daughters in the midst of emotional turmoil is a typical response of those who habitually mother from a distance. However, moms in all styles of mothering may be tempted to ignore their daughters' seemingly unending moodiness, perhaps in the hope that it will just go away. And eventually it will, but chances are that your relationship with your daughter will also wither away as she finds others sources of attention and support.

One mother asked a good question as she lamented to me, "It seems like all my daughter wants is attention. Am I reinforcing the negative emotions by giving her this attention?" Adolescence is a time when our daughters *need* lots of attention, and attention is exactly what we can nourish them with during this once-in-a-lifetime period. The sustenance of our interest and attention can keep our daughters from looking for this attention in all the wrong places.

As far as reinforcing negative emotions is concerned, remember that negative emotions are inevitable. They will come and go during the roller-coaster years of adolescence, whether we pay attention or not. They are more likely, however, to go underground and take root in the dark places of secrecy and withdrawal than they are to come out into the light of our love and attention.

Paying attention with a listening ear and an open heart is a powerful gift to our daughters during their emotional development. The key to listening is *listening to understand.* Unfortunately, many of us are in the habit of listening to be understood. If, in the midst of our daughters' emotional outbursts, we are formulating our response, then we are not listening. One of the most powerful communication techniques a mother can employ is to silently repeat to herself while her daughter is talking, *She really means this.* It doesn't matter whether it's rational, logical, or even right; it is what she is feeling right now.

JUST FOR THE TWO OF YOU

Consider giving your daughter the "gift" of listening. Be creative in packaging this gift. You might want to write it as a declaration, make a poster for her wall, or write it on wallet-size cards for her to put in her purse or backpack. Depending on your daughter's frame of mind (at the moment!), she might think your expression is "hokey" and roll her eyes, but you can be sure she will store your sentiments in her heart and rely on them during stressful times.

Here are a few declarations to get you started:

- "I don't want to listen to just what you say. I want to feel along with you."
- "I won't punish you for your words."
- "I understand that deep emotions are often expressed irrationally."
- "I want you to feel free to say anything."
- "I will listen with my eyes and my ears."
- "I will listen in love."

The poet-philosopher Ralph Waldo Emerson wrote, "It is a luxury to be understood." As we lavish this extravagance of understanding on our daughters, we give them the powerful security of an ally. We send a priceless message: "You are not alone." And together, you and your daughter can find rest in God's promise: "Two are better than one, because they have a good return for their work" (Ecclesiastes 4:9, NIV).

STEREOTYPING VS. TRUSTING

"How can you tell when a teenager is lying? When her lips are moving."

Although one-liners that stereotype teenagers as deceitful, rebellious, or crazy might be funny, they do little to build a bridge of connection between parent and child. In fact, sentiments like this one-liner reinforce the mentality that our children are our enemies. No one has ever been challenged and encouraged toward emotional maturity by being ridiculed or judged. Viewing our daughters negatively or sarcastically will not illuminate the path to emotional maturity, but it will set us up to see our daughters through a lens that will guarantee alliance-splitting conflicts.

A more subtle type of stereotyping is to view our daughters in terms of whoever we dreamed or envisioned they might be. For example, expecting your daughter to have the same temperament as you do or insisting that she follow your interests will break connection between you and her. Our daughters are most likely to develop emotional maturity when they are allowed to develop their own talents and style.

This is where trust comes in. Trusting our children does not mean that we overlook their lies or the foolishnessness that is inevitable in growing up. Some girls become entrenched in deceitfulness and secrecy during adolescence. I am not suggesting that mothers should naively or blindly ignore their daughters' destructive choices. I am suggesting, however, that moms need to hold on to biblical principles of loving well during the turbulence of adolescence more than at any other time.

The apostle Paul described love brilliantly in 1 Corinthians 13 and wrote the best description of a faith-filled vision in verse 6: "[Love] takes pleasure in the flowering of truth." In the Greek language there are two words for time. The first is *chronos,* which describes chronological time—the measure of minutes, hours, days, months, and years. The second is *kairos,* which is translated in the Bible as the "fullness of time." This sense of time describes the blossoming of something when it is ready to flower.

We long for our daughters to be emotionally mature—today. To take pleasure in waiting for this compels us to wait on God and trust in the process of growth. What did we trust when our baby daughters cried, whimpered, and demanded our attention? We trusted that they were expressing themselves appropriately for their age and development and that the sleepless nights, the unexplained crying, and the wailing and whimpering were part of the process of growing up. What can we trust when our teenage daughters are moody, sullen, or withdrawn? We can trust that they are expressing themselves appropriately for their age and development and that the emotional whirlwind is all part of the process of growing up. Sometimes their expressions (although messy and moody) may be cries for help, and we can trust that we are the ones to offer and find help for our daughters. (We will discuss this further in part 3.)

I know that some of you are in the midst of untold agony with your daughters right now, and you don't trust anything—yourself, your daughter, or the process. I urge you to take a few moments right now to find a picture of your daughter when she was a baby or young girl. Close your eyes and remember some of your sweet memories of mothering: Recall the silly, funny things your daughter did or said; think about some of your good times together. You can trust your love for your daughter. It won't eliminate the emotional angst that your daughter is feeling, it won't soothe all the tensions between you, but your love will be your "North Star" during the journey and keep you from becoming angry, bitter, withdrawn, and ineffectual in loving your daughter. To trust in the present, we must see our daughters as they are in God's eyes. "God's glasses are love. Let me put them on first—so that I can see a little of what God sees."[1]

As Jackie, her mother, and I continued to find the disconnectors in their relationship and learn new connecting skills, the going got tough and discouraging. Jackie continued to blame her mother and was skeptical of any attempt by her mother to communicate differently. During one session Jackie hurled these words at her mom: "You're just saying this stuff because we're in Sharon's office. You don't really mean them!" The hurt from her words hung in the air.

"Why do you keep showing up every week?" I asked Jackie's mom. "You get blamed for everything that's gone wrong, and Jackie talks to you with an attitude that, if used with her friends, wouldn't keep them around very long." Jackie quickly looked away from her mom and me and stared at the floor.

Jackie's mom thought for a few moments and then spoke quietly and calmly. "I know Jackie. I know that she doesn't want to be angry and mad at me all the time. I know that I have done some things to contribute to her anger. I believe that if we keep working, we'll figure this out. But even if Jackie stays mad at me, I want to be a better mother."

This was the turning point in our counseling.

CRITICIZING VS. CARING

The responses listed below are all-too-easy "answers" to our daughters' emotional quandaries:

- "You're too sensitive."
- "You've got nothing to cry about."
- "It's not that bad."
- "You're just trying to get attention."
- "Why don't you just get over it?"
- "You're making too much of this."
- "Stop whining."
- "You just like to hear yourself complain."
- "What's wrong with you?"

These responses can leave our daughters feeling judged for their internal realities. Let's face it, it's easy to dismiss or criticize our daughters' emotional complaints. They're sometimes irrational, seem to complain incessantly, and aren't very productive.

It's important for moms to know that teenage girls are capricious in their compassion toward one another. One day they may offer support and sympathy and the next day offer impatience and judgment. My daughter just got home from having lunch with one of her closest friends. She walked into my office and said, "You won't believe what Brittany said to me." I waited for the story. "She said she was surprised I still had a lot of friends since I get into 'my moods' so often." Before I could respond to this common teenage cruelty, Kristin said, "Brittany's one to talk. She's the Queen of Moods."

Teenage girls are quick to recognize moodiness in one another but slow to see their own emotional chaos. Adolescents are sometimes compassionate allies and other times intolerant adversaries, and our consistent response to their emotional turmoil is a key component in helping them develop empathy and kindness toward themselves and others.

One of the most frightening outcomes of the emotional cruelty and the everyday "profaneness" of the adolescent culture is that teens disconnect from their emotional selves. One of my sixteen-year-old clients described it this way: "It's not that you get used to other kids being mean, but by the time you reach your senior year of high school, you learn how to not feel anything. You don't have empathy for anyone."

Although this is not the typical experience for all teenage girls, adolescents live in a culture in which empathy is an unreliable commodity.

When we offer compassion rather than criticism for our daughters' emotional expressions, we provide a two-fold context for connection. We allow our daughters to connect with their emotional selves and learn to respond to themselves appropriately—with comfort, encouragement, challenge, and reason. We also provide a model for our daughters to connect with others with empathy and kindness. Researcher and writer Patricia Evans describes one reality of teenage culture: "Many boys and girls suffer the dehumanizing and devastating loss of their emotional awareness [due to subtle and overt verbal assaults]."[2]

We mothers have an opportunity, in the midst of our daughters' relationships with their unpredictable and unreliable peers, to offer something different—to connect with compassion and restore emotional awareness as part of the process of developing emotional maturity.

Below are some connecting sentences of caring to use instead of the disconnecting sentences of criticism listed above:
- "You're feeling a lot."
- "It sounds like a lot is going on right now."
- "Things look pretty bad right now, don't they?"
- "What's the pain you're feeling right now?"
- "I know this is what you're feeling right now."
- "I know this is important to you."
- "What else are you feeling right now?"
- "Is there anything else you'd like to tell me?"
- "It makes sense that you would feel this way."

If you're tempted to think, *If I express caring without commentary, my daughter will think it's okay to whine, complain, and be moody,* remember that our daughters are moved toward emotional maturity not by our controlling them, but by our hearts toward them. A critical heart is interested in reforming or remaking our daughters. A compassionate heart is committed to the transformation that can occur in the midst of emotional expression as our daughters realize they can trust us.

As Jackie's mom continued to express empathy and concern for her daughter's complaints, Jackie's resistance began to crumble. I envisioned Jackie's mom as a soldier wearing a bulletproof vest of love and commitment to her relationship with her daughter. She took a lot of "bullets" from Jackie.

If Jackie's mom had defended herself against Jackie's criticism and criticized her daughter in return, they would have remained entrenched in the warfare of blame. But Jackie's mom responded with caring humility, and in response Jackie looked at me, shrugged her shoulders, and said, "I guess some of this is my fault, too." I wanted to shout "Victory!" but I knew we still had a long way to go.

THREATENING VS. NEGOTIATING

"I can't take it anymore," Jackie's mom said in despair only a few sessions after our breakthrough session. "It's just not getting any better. If I'm such a bad mom, maybe Jackie should find someone else to be her mother."

Mothers everywhere can understand this mom's veiled threat. Although we don't always say it aloud, we think about running away, resigning, or maybe joining the circus. (Taming lions would be a breeze after mothering an adolescent!)

Other threatening responses to emotional expression might sound like this: "When you can calm down, I'll talk to you," or "If you don't stop complaining, we can't talk." Threats are always an ineffectual way of communicating and immediately break connection. Relationships crumble under pressure, and threats, demands, and ultimatums are a source of pressure. This doesn't mean that sometimes it isn't better to wait until after the emotional storm has passed to have a meaningful conversation.

There are two important principles for "negotiating" during conversations with our daughters. First, affirm the emotion you or your daughter is feeling, and second, set a time for reconnection. If your daughter needs a time-out to get a handle on her anger or withdrawal, set a specific time and location to get together again. You might say, "I know you're really angry right now, so let's get together in an hour and see if you feel like taking a walk or going to get ice cream." If you are angry or feeling something that might keep you from being helpful to your daughter (moms have "off" times too), you might say, "This is not a good time for me to talk, so let's have breakfast together in the morning and continue this conversation."

Okay, go ahead and be honest. Some of you are thinking, *This lady has her head in the clouds. She doesn't know half the names my daughter has called me! Am I supposed to be a doormat and coddle my daughter when she's behaving badly?*

JUST FOR YOU

As moms we do not have unlimited emotional resources, and our adolescent daughters can tax us to our limits. It's important for us to take spontaneous time-outs or schedule time for ourselves to replenish our own emotional reserves. Add your own sources of emotional sustenance to the following list:

- Take a long soak in a candlelit bubble bath.
- Read a portion of the Psalms.
- Have your own movie night. Don't forget the popcorn!
- Schedule a date with your husband.
- Take a girls' night out with your girlfriends.
- Get a manicure or pedicure (or give yourself one).
- Turn on your car radio and tune in to the music you like.
- Clean out your bedroom closet.
- Take a long walk.
- Spend time doing a favorite hobby or craft.

- _____.
- _____.
- _____.
- _____.

If your relationship with your daughter is in a particularly volatile season or if she has a short fuse that results in an explosion and leaves you lying in debris, then setting boundaries is especially important for you. You can set boundaries and impose consequences for bad behavior without threatening or breaking connection completely.

BLAMING VS. BEFRIENDING

We've already mentioned the natural tendency to blame each other during the tension of emotional turbulence. A good antidote for a heart of blame is a heart to befriend your daughter.

Now I agree with the parenting experts who suggest that we live in a culture of parents who are afraid to be the parents and simply want to be their children's friends. One of the most important roles of mothering is to provide a sense of security and safety, and this comes in part from setting strong boundaries and using discipline. But security and safety are not completely satisfied by rules and regulations; they are also fostered when our daughters know that we enjoy them.

Whom do you feel the safest with? I suspect it is with those who know you, allow you to be yourself, and enjoy your quirks and eccentricities. Our

JUST FOR THE TWO OF YOU

Block out an hour or two on your calendar to practice friendship. The purpose of these dates with your daughter is solely to enjoy each other. Do something you both take pleasure in: Take a walk, hike, drive, or go to a special restaurant. Make it a rule not to bring up any unpleasant subjects during these times. Practice having fun, being comfortable together, and making each other feel good.

Moms, you will probably have to take the lead in scheduling these times and sticking to them, but as your daughter learns that she can trust these times as a safety zone of fun and enjoyment, she may start to suggest dates of her own.

daughters are no different than we are. They long for the safety and security of our enjoyment of them.

We resort to blame when we forget that the way our teenagers develop independence and self-reliance is by turning against us. We can't take it personally! We can befriend our daughters when we remember that we are the parents and our job is to never turn against them.

SPIRITUALIZING VS. SPIRITUALLY GUIDING

It can be hard for those of us who rely on our faith to guide and sustain us to acknowledge that our spiritual platitudes can dismiss and even betray our daughters. Spiritualizing our daughters' emotional experiences can discount their feelings, and sounding self-righteous or preachy can denigrate their experiences and break our emotional connection. Platitudes often pour automatically from the mouths of well-meaning mothers. Phrases like "God will work everything out," "We just have to trust God to take care of things," or "God doesn't like an angry spirit" are ineffectual at best and shaming at worst. Our daughters may get the feeling that they are "bad" to feel negative emotions, and as a result they may not only hide their feelings from us but shut themselves off from God as well. Spiritual platitudes don't address the problem and may create more pain in the very people they are intended to soothe.

Spiritually guiding our daughters toward emotional growth, on the other hand, begins with believing ourselves that suffering can move us toward God. How we deal with emotional turmoil depends largely on our ability to see what the experience of suffering can do in our hearts. "We are faced with the

JUST FOR YOU

Read through Psalms. Notice the full range of emotions expressed by the psalmists. You might even want to note in the margin of your Bible the specific emotions expressed. As mothers after God's own heart, we are called to be present in the midst of the gamut of our daughters' emotional expressions just as God is present with us in the midst of all we feel.

challenge of learning how to wrestle with sorrow so that it can bring about the greatest good."[3]

Our daughters' emotional growth provides the best context for us to learn to trust God and rely on His love for us, even when we feel doubt, anger, and sadness. The wonder of God's love is that He created us to feel and express *all* our emotions so that we might better experience all He feels for us. Our aim is not to keep our daughters from feeling any emotion by offering spiritual platitudes. Rather, we should seek to "gently brush away the dust from [our children's] glory, so that we both may stare in awe at what God has already made."[4]

Part II

Building a Bridge
Between Your Worlds

If your most deeply held desire is to know God, to make all that you do an act of worship, then the guidance you give your child will be more like the light touch of a butterfly on a flower than the heavy hand of domination that "breaks the will" of a weaker ego. Rather than dispensing rules, regulations, and righteousness, you seek to assist your child to see the path clearly. After all, we are all on this journey together.

—HUGH AND GAYLE PRATHER, *Spiritual Parenting*

Chapter 5

"Mom, I'm Not in the Mood!"

[Ninety percent] of high school girls admit that they've thought they were crazy.

—Kimberly Dawn Neumann, "The Jump on Body and Soul"

It's a relief, isn't it? Teenage girls think that they might be crazy. That suspicion doesn't come as a surprise to the families of adolescent girls. Trusted author and therapist Mary Pipher assures us,

> A friend once told me that the best way to understand teenagers was to think of them as constantly on LSD. It was good advice. People on acid are intense, changeable, internal, often cryptic or uncommunicative and, of course, dealing with a different reality. That's all true for adolescent girls.[1]

Perhaps you've experienced (or should I say survived) the "different reality" of your daughter, only to catch your breath and realize that you are yet again in a different reality. Sometimes siblings bear the brunt of the mood change, as Kristin's younger brother, Graham, did one day when we were all washing the dishes.

Kristin was complaining about one of her friends. "She is so moody," Kristin lamented. "She goes from being happy to yelling and screaming, all in the same five minutes."

Kristin described her friend with uncanny precision and with a light-heartedness that tricked her brother. Graham innocently moved into the conversation. "I thought she seemed a little wacko," Graham suggested in the same teasing tone as his sister's.

Kristin slammed the pan she was drying onto the counter and looked at her brother with daggers in her eyes. "How dare you criticize one of my friends?" she yelled. "She is a good person, and you are mean. Mom, tell him to be nice."

I forgot that Kristin was in a different reality and thought that I would just be reasonable. "Kristin," I began, "you were the one who started being critical of your friend. Graham was just trying to add to the conversation."

Big mistake. Kristin dissolved into tears. "Everyone in this family gangs up on me. You are always on Graham's side. I can't say anything right. Mom, I am not in the mood to deal with this right now!"

Graham and I looked at each other, both feeling a bit like deer caught in the headlights. Thank goodness the telephone rang and interrupted this conversation that was only going downhill.

Kristin noted on caller ID that the telephone call was one of her friends. "I'll take it," she snapped, as she grabbed the phone and wiped away a tear. "Oh hi, Dana!" Her voice changed immediately. "You won't believe what happened today in English," she continued. "It was so great…"

Graham and I continued to look at each other with disbelief. *What just happened?* Graham started to leave the room, and then paused. "Remind me to never talk to my sister again."

The emotional climate in adolescent girls is extreme and changeable. It is somewhat of a relief to know that there is a biological reason for this. As the brain develops, the neurons that register emotion are developing as well. As previously mentioned in chapter 3, emotions (especially sadness) trigger neurons in an area that is eight times larger in the female brain than in the male brain.[2]

That explains some things, doesn't it? You are not crazy. As your daughter enters adolescence, you join her on a roller-coaster ride that quickly crosses over from being exhilarating and surprising to being frustrating and terrifying. Imagine for a moment what your emotional world would be like if you felt everything eight times more intensely than you feel it right now. (Although not a specific scientific explanation, this is an accurate extrapolation.) You might seem a little crazy yourself.

In this chapter we will look at the moodiness of teenage girls and use the world-bridging insights and strategies from the past four chapters to develop a response to our daughters that will keep us all from losing our minds as well as provide a context for our daughters to grow toward emotional maturity.

MOOD SHOPPING

Take a twelve- or thirteen-year-old girl shopping, and you are in for an interesting time. Girls on the cusp of adolescence are trying to find their own style, and a shopping trip reveals the multitude of styles that there are to pick from. Kristin and I laugh when we look back at her middle-school pictures. For a time she wore big bangs, and her hair had enough hair spray on it to meet the spray-net needs of an entire town's population. She went through a very blue eye-shadow phase, a time when she wore only sweat pants and T-shirts, and a time when she pushed the limits by wearing midriff-baring shirts and short shorts. Moms who have experience with teenagers know that if they express shock at a particular style of dress or disgust for certain hairstyles or makeup techniques, they will ensure that their daughters will pick those very styles!

Moods have a lot in common with fashion styles. As our daughters enter adolescence and experience the changes in their developing brains that allow

JUST FOR THE TWO OF YOU

Keep a stash of fashion magazines or catalogs on hand for the purpose of building a connection with your daughter. Set aside time for the two of you to flip through a magazine together. Ask your daughter to mark outfits or fashions that are appealing to her. Go back through the magazine and look at what she marked. Ask her if an outfit or style reflects a particular mood. Resist the urge to criticize or comment on the appropriateness of the style; instead, use your daughter's preference to get to know her better. As you relax your grip on your daughter's fashion choices, you will discover that styles are transitory and will change. Don't let your relationship pay for the trendy or foolish style of the moment. The same goes for your daughter's moods. They will come and go. As you relax your grip on trying to control her moods, you will be freer to embrace your daughter.

them to feel a broader and more intense range of emotions, they have the opportunity to "try on" a lot of different moods. A girl who was even-tempered and had a bright, sunny personality during childhood discovers that she can feel angry and sad. A girl who seemed carefree as a child discovers brooding and outrage. The new moods may even be reflected in a new mode of dress. Girls who were content to play in overalls and bright-colored clothing want to wear black pants and shirts and black leather jewelry with scary metal spikes sticking out of it. Girls who painted their fingernails pink and begged to play with their mom's makeup try on black fingernail polish and makeup styles that their moms would never imagine, much less wear themselves.

When we respond to our daughters' moods with surprise or disgust, much like our knee-jerk reactions to their fashion experiments, we may unwittingly encourage them to pick a particular mood as their style of relating. Moods are emotions that our daughters try on as a natural part of growing up and finding their own style. When we use our daughters' moods—as extreme or unreasonable as they may be—as an opportunity to connect with them and cheer them on to emotional maturity, we diffuse the power of moods to take over and control both our daughters and us.

FEELING "So Much"

Amanda's parents brought her to see me because she was in trouble with the law. Amanda had gone on a little shoplifting spree at a local grocery store. Security cameras caught her on videotape, and store officials stopped her before she left the store, then called her parents and the police.

Amanda's parents could not make sense of her explanation for the shop-lifting. Amanda had always been a "good girl." She had started to change in adolescence, wearing dark clothing all the time and wanting to pierce her eye-brow, but her parents never thought she would break the law.

"I can't explain it either, really," Amanda told me. "I just got in this mood that was restless and bored, and when I went to the store with my friends, someone suggested that we steal some stuff. So I did." Amanda's explanation that she shoplifted because of a mood did not sit well with her parents, so they brought her to me.

"I'll bet this isn't the first weird mood you've had lately," I suggested to

Amanda. My comment unleashed story after story about moods of anger, sadness, and irritability. Amanda talked about feeling "so much" and not being able to make sense of it. I asked Amanda to spend some time every day during the next week writing down every negative thought she had, and I shared the assignment with Amanda's mom. She looked perplexed and frightened.

"Can you talk about what you're feeling?" I asked Amanda's mom.

"I don't know if it's such a good idea for Amanda to think more about her negative feelings," she explained. "I thought maybe we should focus on more positive feelings. Isn't it the negative feelings that are starting to get Amanda into trouble?"

Her question was a good one, and it is the natural response of mothers to their daughters when they start to experience scary moods and even scarier behaviors. But it is not a response that encourages relationship or leads toward emotional maturity. In the last chapter we looked at the disconnecting responses of denial and ignoring. I wanted to encourage Amanda to become aware of the thoughts behind the moods and encourage her mother to be curious and listen.

When Amanda came in for her next visit, she shared some of her thoughts with me. One theme I noticed in her expressions was that of feeling she didn't fit in. She shared that everyone else but her seemed to have a best friend. She felt as if everyone else knew a secret language of belonging that she didn't know. She concluded that she didn't know the right "look," the right way of being with others, or the right words to say to connect. I asked Amanda if she would share with her mother some of what she had written and talked about with me.

When Amanda's mother joined us, Amanda tried to describe her feelings. "I just feel like a dork," Amanda began. "I hate my clothes and the way my hair looks. I have zits all over my forehead."

Amanda's mom responded immediately. "We've tried to give you everything you want. We took you to a dermatologist, and he said that your acne was 'typical adolescent acne.' I don't know what else we can do." Amanda's mom broke connection by denying Amanda's feelings while justifying her own behavior. She didn't even have time to think about being curious, listening, caring, or befriending because she took Amanda's moodiness personally.

Letting Go

It is impossible to connect with our daughters when we take their moodiness personally. It seems that at the moment of our daughters' greatest moodiness, a desperate defensiveness rises up within us. We make a valiant attempt to save ourselves in response to our daughter's moods. It makes sense to respond to their outrage, anger, sadness, or even giddiness by shrinking back from them and defending ourselves.

When our daughters are in a mood, there are two paths we can take that will encourage them toward emotional maturity. One path is to help them find the thought behind the mood and confront it, affirm it, answer it, or pray about it. For example, the thoughts behind Amanda's mood of restlessness were about not belonging or fitting in. Amanda's mom might have

Just for You

The next time you take your daughter's moodiness personally, set some time aside for your own transformative work.

Identify as many of your responses to your daughter as you can. Write down all the distressing thoughts you may have about your daughter. Then divide your thoughts into those that blame or criticize your daughter and those that defend yourself.

Let go of your critical and defensive thoughts by writing what is true about your daughter, or what you hope to be true, and what is true about yourself, or what you would like to be true.

The following excerpt is from Amanda's mom's journal (used with her permission).

Amanda	*Me*
Ungrateful	Giving Amanda all she wants
Self-absorbed	Don't have any more to give
Too focused on appearance	Never say the right thing
Low self-esteem	Low self-esteem

asked, "Is there a time when you felt like you did fit in? What was going on then?" Or "Tell me more about the frustrations of being in a group that is so superficially focused on appearances."

Of course, these kinds of exchanges can be tricky outside the therapeutic setting. My daughter has chastised me when I've tried to ask probing questions. "Mom, I don't want to be 'therapized' right now!"

All we can do is invite our daughters to talk further about their feelings. If our daughters brush us off, we can gather our wits about us and wait for another opportunity to invite connection with curiosity and compassion. (In the meantime, it's not a bad idea to nurse your hurt feelings with a little TLC—a walk with a good friend or a really good cup of coffee!) When we take things personally, we feel offended and react to defend ourselves, which will inevitably create disconnection or conflict.

Transformation:

Amanda	*Me*
Needy and grateful	Generous
Focused on others	Want to be available for Amanda
Appearance is important, but so are internal values	Don't care about saying the right thing, just about loving Amanda
Developing self-confidence	Developing self-confidence

I could tell Amanda I understand that she lives in a world that places a lot of importance on appearance and ask if there's anything (else) that we can do to increase her confidence. I can tell her about my college experience and how the focus began to shift from just being "pretty" to being a person of substance. I can make it a point to compliment Amanda on her appearance and her demonstrations of character.

Amanda's mom told me that this exercise increased her compassion for her daughter and her confidence in herself. It didn't make Amanda's mood change, but it allowed her mom to let go of having to control that mood in the moment and reminded her to believe in where the mood might lead Amanda in the future.

The second path we can walk (or crawl) with our daughters is to encourage them to be transformed in spite of their moods. This is hard work, and it is essential that we have done some of this transformative work on our own before we can hope to help our daughters. Our daughters' moodiness is a perfect opportunity for our own transformation. If Amanda's mom scrambles to defend herself when Amanda is feeling insecure and restless, there is no possibility for transformation for either mother or daughter. If, however, Amanda's mom can remember who she is in the moment—a mother of compassion and wisdom, and a woman who has struggled with belonging and found her own sense of self—she can point Amanda toward transformation. She might say, "There is no feeling worse than not fitting in. I am so sorry for what you are feeling." Or "I remember a job situation where I felt like I didn't fit in with any of the other women. I decided to focus on my own abilities and strengths and work to feel good about myself on the job, and gradually I noticed that I was developing good relationships with others."

[Letting go] means that you pray and suffer and hang on and give things up and hope and sweat.

—THOMAS MERTON, *New Seeds of Contemplation*

Once again, our daughters may roll their eyes and seem to dismiss our experience. Remember, however, that being curious about our daughters or inviting them to change is not *only* about their response to us. If our daughters' responses dictate our interactions with them, we will be tempted to become mute! When we take things personally, we cannot see our daughters as they really are, and we cannot see ourselves accurately either. When we have to defend ourselves, we cannot offer ourselves.

As you offer your daughter curiosity and compassionately nudge her toward transformation, she may remain entrenched in her mood. She may need a few hours or days or even years to process the conversation and gradually respond over time. But in the process, you will most assuredly become more of who you want to be: an intentional, inviting mother of fierce compassion.

Finding a Focus

One of the traps we fall into when it comes to our daughters' moodiness is that we tend to focus on the mood, and the result is that we spend our daughters' adolescence surviving their mood of the moment rather than focusing on their emotional growth.

Once again, there are two paths we can take that lead to emotional maturity. The first path is to look at the mood in the moment and then ask ourselves what we want for our daughters and why.

For example, when our daughter says, "I'm not in the mood to clean my room," what do we want at that moment? A clean room. Why? Because we are having guests over, or simply because a clean house is important to us. Then we say, "I understand you don't feel like cleaning your room. Could you just straighten things up before our guests come, or could you make your bed every other day because it's important to me?" Remember to negotiate, be compassionate, and befriend your daughter. You could agree that she can indulge her mood for a week and that you will too for that matter! (Did you know that 79 percent of Americans *don't* make their beds every day?)[3]

The second path of response to your daughter's moodiness is to focus on future growth and emotional development. When your daughter says, "I'm not in the mood to go to church," you can begin by being curious about the thoughts behind this mood. Perhaps your daughter is struggling in relationships at church or is questioning her own faith.

Respect: "admiration, courtesy, regard"
Honor: "esteem, kudos, praise"

—The Oxford English Dictionary

Remember that denial, criticism, or intimidation will break connection. Resist the inclination to say, "We go to church in this family. You'll get up and go whether you like it or not." If it's important to you for your daughter to go to church, tell her why, that you want to be together as a family, that your church is important to you, that you've made a commitment. Negotiate. You might negotiate a once-a-month "pass" with your daughter when she could either stay home one Sunday morning or miss one youth group meeting per month, but the rest of the time she would go. Remind your daughter (and yourself) that it is possible for everyone to get what she or he wants. The cycle works like this: When Mom and Dad are respected and honored, they are more likely to give additional and increasing privileges. When a daughter is respected and honored, she is more likely to give respect and honor. Renegotiate as often as necessary.

Does the idea of negotiating sound too indulgent or potentially exhausting? It is hard work to develop a growing relationship with your daughter in the midst of her emotional immaturity. There will be times when you can say, "I'm too tired (or frustrated or busy) to negotiate this with you right now.

Just for You

Perspective takes practice. Practice looking at your daughter's moods with a two-way mirror. Look at what you want for her in the moment, and then what you long for her to experience in future growth and development. When you feel a bit more confident in your response, begin to "practice" with your daughter. She may resist at first, but as you persist in finding perspective in the midst of her moodiness, your view of her moods will give your daughter security and focus.

Mood	In the Moment	In the Future
Anger at peers	Not hurt herself or others	Be mobilized to action or uncover sadness
Apathy about school	Pass her classes	Love learning, find interests
Jealous of sister	Get along with sister	Enjoy her sister and believe in her and see her own beauty and talents

You can add to this chart as you identify your own daughter's moods and what you want for her in the moment and in the future.

You will just have to do what I ask, and we will negotiate this the next time." Remind your daughter that she will get more of what she wants as she gives you respect and consideration. When she does "give" on her wants or defer to you, let her see the payoff big time!

Kristin began begging for a later curfew the day she turned sixteen. We talked, discussed, and debated about curfews almost every weekend. I told Kristin I wasn't ready to extend her curfew and that I would let her know when I was ready to negotiate. The next weekend when she made plans to go out with friends, she didn't ask for an extended curfew. She even came home a few minutes early, kissed me good night, and happily went off to bed. The next weekend I was ready to discuss extending her curfew to an hour later. When I gave her the privilege, I thanked her for honoring me the prior weekend and reminded her that negotiation is not just about words. In fact, the most effective negotiating tool is respectful behavior.

That addresses the moment, but what about future development? In the previous example about church attendance, you might ask your daughter to write or talk about the function church has served in her life up until this point and how she will pay attention to and honor her spiritual life in the future. If she resists, tell her that you want to honor her changing opinions about church, but that you need her to honor them as well by thinking about them, articulating them, and developing them. Ask your daughter what it's like for her to go to church just for your sake, and tell her what it would mean to you if she would participate in church as a gift to the family.

Chances are that your daughter's immediate response will be, "I don't want to talk about it. I'm not in the mood!" Remember that she is trying on this mood, and your response might determine its appeal. In the moment you can respond, "I know that's how moods feel. They grab you in the moment, and it's not a good time to talk. Let's talk about your inclination to stop going to church in the morning." Let her wear the mood for now. You can talk about it later.

What if your daughter says she doesn't care about you and what you want? Take a deep breath, and *don't take it personally*. Pull the offer to negotiate off the table and simply state: "When you're ready to invest in getting what you want, you will begin to experience the payoff. Just let me know." No pouting, silent treatment, or further words are necessary.

One mom I know negotiated with a brilliance that would outshine the experts on Wall Street. Every time she said no to her daughter's request about a social activity, her daughter would throw a fit. She would yell, threaten, and eventually storm off to her room. Each time that happened, her mom reminded her that her behavior squashed the chance for future negotiations. She suggested that the next time she said no, her daughter might calmly respond, "Remember you said no last time too. Is there any way we could negotiate this?"

It took nearly a year for her daughter to regulate her own emotions enough to remember the concept of negotiation. She continued to get mad, blow up, and not get her way for ten solid months. Her mom described the turning point to me. Her daughter asked to go to a late movie with a group of friends. Her mom said no, citing the need to be at church early the next morning as the reason. Her daughter reminded her, "Last weekend you said no too. Would you please reconsider? I'll do anything I can to help you get everyone else ready for church in the morning."

> *One of the greatest gifts I would receive [from my child]: the*
> *understanding that the word mother is more powerful when*
> *it is used as a verb than as a noun.*
>
> —MARTHA BECK, *Expecting Adam*

This mother almost jumped up and down for joy as she granted permission to her daughter. You can bet there will be many negotiations ahead and probably a few more noes and temper tantrums.

This exhausting and relentless task of negotiation during the adolescent years is no less important or rewarding than the previous tasks of teaching your daughter to tie her shoes, ride her bike, write her letters, and memorize her multiplication tables. You will get tired and discouraged, but don't give up. You are guiding your daughter toward emotional maturity.

TAKING HEART

One afternoon years ago I slipped into Kristin's bedroom while she was napping to watch her sleep. (My mother advised me that when I felt like I was going to lose it during those terrible twos and threes, I should spend a few minutes watching my sleeping child before I decided to run away. It's a good practice during the tumultuous teenage years as well!) Kristin had kicked off her fuzzy pink blanket, and her bare feet poked out at the end of her bed. As I pulled her blanket to cover her, I noticed that she was holding a half-eaten watermelon lollipop—one we had bought as a treat earlier at the grocery store. Now it made a pink splotch on her pillowcase; it had specks of pink fuzz from the blanket on it, not to mention a few strands of Kristin's hair. Yuck.

I did what any mother would do. I pried back Kristin's fingers one by one, freed the sucker from her grasp, and threw it away. When Kristin awoke from her nap, she ran to me with a singleness of purpose. "Where is my watermelon sucker?" I'll never forget Kristin's response when I explained my well-meaning and reasonable actions. "But it was *mine*. I wasn't ready to throw it away."

I remember the watermelon sucker when I am tempted to try to pry Kristin's moods from her grasp, and I pray for the patience and courage to let her *become*. As we let go of taking our daughters' moodiness personally and find perspective in the midst of the changing emotions, we must hold on to the belief that our daughters are becoming.

Becoming what? You may fear at times that your daughter is becoming something that might need to be locked up for a very long time! It's hard to resist pulling our daughters from the messiness or wanting to clean up all the sticky yuckiness. It is our life's work as mothers, however, to be patient and nurture all that is within our daughters with love and attentiveness.

When our daughters snarl, threaten to run away, and scream that they hate us, we will need to look at something other than our daughters to remember who they are becoming, who they are meant to be. We need to wrap the words of the apostle Paul around our hearts: "We fix our eyes not on what is seen, but on what is unseen. For what is seen is temporary, but what is unseen is eternal" (2 Corinthians 4:18, NIV).

Look at your daughter's baby pictures, allow yourself to dream of all you long for her to be, and pray that God will give you a vision of who she is becoming. This takes courage. Courage comes from the French word *coeur*, which means "heart." To let go and find perspective, we have to "take heart."

Taking heart will look different for every mother and daughter, but it will involve certain realities for all. Foundational to taking heart as we wait is to patiently and passionately believe in our daughters' becoming. Perhaps you can recall when you were eight months pregnant, and then eight months and one day, eight months and one week, eight months and two weeks. Perhaps you had days, as I did, when you were certain that you would be the first woman in history to be pregnant forever. Waiting for your daughter to be born (or waiting to adopt) was as excruciating as the actual physical birth pains.

You will feel the pain again as your daughter is being born into emotional maturity. That's what you hope she's being born into, anyway! What if she's not? Just as in the first labor and delivery, you had limited control over the outcome, so now you can only faithfully labor and wait for the outcome. Wait with patience and with passion. Be patient as your daughter tries on outlandish or even scary moods; she is being born. Be passionate about who you long for your daughter to become.

RISKING BECOMING

I will never forget the mother who came to see me with her eighth-grade daughter after she had cut her hair herself and died it pink. I could hardly take my eyes off the girl—much as I can't turn my eyes away from a horrible traffic accident along the side of the road! Her mother's words shifted my perspective. "I'm so excited about the creative, courageous girl my daughter is becoming," she said. "I've enrolled her in the design class at the Art Institute of Colorado. Don't you think she has talent?" This mom was willing to wait passionately through pink hair for her daughter to become so much more!

Taking heart involves not only waiting with patience and passion, but it means risking as if our daughters' becoming were already true. What if you responded to your daughter as if she were already the young woman you long for her to be and believe God has created her to be? This, of course, requires faith. The writer to the Hebrews described faith as "being sure of what we hope for and certain of what we do not see" (Hebrews 11:1, NIV). What if you responded to your daughter's moodiness as if she were full of wisdom, compassion, gratitude, insight, confidence, and purpose? You might seem a little crazy yourself.

Mothering our daughters "by heart" means risking that there's more here than meets the eye. When your daughter yells at you, stomps her feet, and slams the door to her room, can you look beyond the present and, with a faith-filled heart, trust that she is becoming a young woman of passion and purpose? It may seem that she is just becoming a brat. You may need to interrupt her outburst or enforce consequences for disrespectful behavior. But you can learn to stop and pray for her before you react. Or maybe you'll remark when she comes out of her room, "Wow, you are filled with passion. It is amazing to watch."

Before you jump to the conclusion that I'm a permissive parent who is missing an opportunity to discipline and instruct, ask yourself which has been most effective in your own life: when someone reacts to your moodiness and bad behavior with disapproval or a lecture, or when someone sees past your moodiness and bad behavior with a vision of who you could become? As our daughters grow into adolescence, our real power is less in ruling them in the moment and more in trusting who they are becoming.

Have you ever wondered what keeps God from intervening in the midst of all our foolishness *right now* and putting an end to our misery and the misery we create? He sees more than swirling chaos. Thomas Merton expressed it this way: "You have willed to see me more really as I am. For the sinful self is not my real self, it is not the self You have wanted for me, only the self I have wanted for myself. And I no longer want this false self."[4]

God, make a fresh start in me, shape a Genesis week
from the chaos of my life.

—Psalm 51:10

Let me give you a picture of a risk-taking mom by finishing Amanda's story. As Amanda's mom began to see and change her own disconnecting habits, she began to believe more and more in who Amanda was becoming. A by-product of mothering with positive intentions is that our focus becomes less and less negative, even in the midst of negative emotions. Amanda's mom risked believing that although Amanda was feeling insecure and out of place, she was becoming a young woman of empathy for others and of far greater depth than the superficial concerns of the teenage culture.

Amanda's mom signed their family up to sponsor a needy child overseas and encouraged Amanda to draw pictures, write notes, and send gifts to this child. She allowed Amanda to pierce her eyebrow and paint her fingernails black and supported her in wanting to be different from her shallow peers. She brainstormed with Amanda and one of her friends about doing something different for the Christmas season. She waited through stormy moods and believed in more than the storm.

Amanda expressed an interest in doing something for homeless kids during the holidays. Her mother encouraged her creativity on behalf of those who don't belong. Amanda solicited families in the neighborhood and got donations of blankets and socks. She and a friend packaged the donations with homemade cookies, and on Christmas Eve they distributed the packages to homeless kids and their families.

Since Christmas Amanda has continued to experience a broad range of moods. She's felt "yucky" about herself and complained about everyone else. But when she tries on these moods, her mother remembers (and sometimes reminds Amanda) of what she "wore" on Christmas Eve. The memory gives them hope for the future and a picture of one "outfit" that really fit!

[Christ's love is] marked by giving, not getting. Christ's love makes the church whole. His words evoke her beauty. Everything he does and says is designed to bring the best out of her, dressing her in dazzling white silk, radiant with holiness.

—EPHESIANS 5:25-27

Chapter 6

"Mom, Just Leave Me Alone!"

Girls fight with body language and relationships instead of fists and knives. There is no gesture more devastating than the back turning away.

—Rachel Simmons, *Odd Girl Out*

It's the secret we mothers keep from one another: *Our daughters can be mean to us.*

I guess we shouldn't be surprised. We yelled at our mothers, slammed our bedroom doors, and muttered "I hate you" under our breath. Still, it is shocking to feel the cold stare or hear the harsh words of our little girls— directed at us. Admitting the truth makes us anxious. What does it mean that our daughters are capable of such relational atrocities? In a society that encourages us to raise girls to be loving and nice, it is extremely disconcerting to acknowledge that our daughters are at times hateful and mean.

One mother bravely disclosed her story to me. What's funny is that it is really a common story that most mothers and daughters have experienced. What's sad is that it is often a secret story that mothers are afraid to tell, fearing that it might reveal their daughters to be monsters and themselves to be pitiful failures.

"Libby, how was your day?" this mother asked routinely.

"I don't want to talk about it, especially with you." Libby's words surprised and stung her mother.

"Why not? I want to know what's going on with you."

"You are the last person I want to talk to. You'll probably just lecture me anyway." Libby's coldness froze her mother's heart.

"I promise I won't. Tell me what's going on with you," Libby's mother pleaded.

"I said I don't want to talk about it. Just leave me alone."

And with a final look toward her mother that would have stopped the most hardhearted criminal, Libby left the room.

Libby's mother shared with me that she was tempted to run after her daughter, begging for her presence, while at the same time wanting to just slug her! There is no more difficult time to mother with wisdom, compassion, and intentionality than in the midst of our adolescent daughters' coldness, cruelty, and withdrawal. Nor is there a more crucial time to mother! Our daughters' cold glares and cutting words provide the perfect opportunity for us to teach them about self-esteem, committed relationships, and authentic personal power.

But before we can do that, we must understand the hidden meanings in their angst-filled words and rejecting behaviors. Your daughter's cry, "Just leave me alone!" is a code that contains clues to her painful relational experiences. If you become a good "sleuth," you can learn to mother well even in the face of aggression or rejection. Your daughter's withdrawal or hostility can also provide an excellent opportunity to teach her about her legitimate need for privacy and help her develop positive self-regard. "Mom, just leave me alone!" can be your cue to guide your daughter toward authentic power during a time when she feels so powerless that she is lashing out at the safest and most intimate relationship she has—her relationship with you.

DECODING THE PAIN

When your daughter screams hateful words at you and retreats to her bedroom (after slamming the door), you have just experienced *relational aggression.* Yes, there's a name for it. And no, that won't ease the pain. However, understanding relational aggression can help you decode your daughter's painful experiences in relationships. Studies suggest that by the time girls are three years old, they are more relationally aggressive than boys! Researchers describe "common angry, hurtful…behavior enacted in girls' peer groups… through damage to relationships or feelings of acceptance, friendships, or group inclusion."[1]

We don't need scientists to tell us what we have all experienced. In my first book *Bravehearts: Unlocking the Courage to Love with Abandon,* I write of my own first experience with relational aggression on the playground:

The girls in this…school played a game during recess in which they would join hands and chant: *Tick, tock. The game is locked and nobody else can play with us. But if you do, we'll take your shoe and keep it for a week or two.*

I remember watching them play and looking down at my black-and-white Buster Brown shoes as I listened over and over to every word. I looked longingly at the girls in the game…. I waited for the glorious invitation to clasp hands and sing out the rhyming words that would signify: "I have friends. I belong. I'm part of The Girls."

I don't remember how many days I waited—it seemed like decades to a seven-year-old—until I could not possibly wait one more day. During a cold and snowy recess, I walked across the playground to greet the ringleader of The Girls. I presented her my slightly scuffed Buster Brown shoe and delivered the eloquent speech I'd practiced all the way to school: *"I want to play."*

She looked at me in amazement. To this day, I don't know if it was the fact that someone actually listened to their chant and took them at their words or if it was my undarned sock with big toe peeking through on the snowy blacktop that caused her astonished glare![2]

Just for You

1. Recall your earliest experiences in relationships. What did they teach you about yourself and relationships?
2. Think about a time when you felt you did not belong. What emotions characterized this time? Anger? Sadness? Loneliness?
3. What do you wish others (your parents, your friends, your siblings, your roommates) would have said or done for you?
4. Think about a time when you felt you did belong. Who or what contributed to this sense of belonging?

Since I wrote that story, I have heard hundreds of stories from women about events that took place on playgrounds, at slumber parties, or in school cafeterias—stories that have revealed the desire to belong and the uniquely female practices of exclusion and inclusion. Our yearning to belong is evidence of our design for relationships. Our stories of not belonging are evidence that we humans don't do relationships perfectly—not even close.

We understand that we must practice a musical instrument in order to play well, we must practice cooking if we want to serve a gourmet feast, and we must practice a sport if we want to coordinate our movements with the rules of the game. But no one tells us that we have to practice mothering. In order to live the principles of hand-in-hand mothering, you must practice. So must I. Decoding our daughters' pain and its resulting negative behavior takes work and wisdom. Honesty, maturity, kindness, and invitation don't come naturally in the midst of mothering a teenager. Fear, hurt, defensiveness, and pouting are more the natural responses for me.

When your daughter pushes you away, she is often transferring what she feels or fears from her peers. She may be acting out toward you the inner tension she feels because of problems at home—a difficult sibling, her parents' troubled marriage, or the family's financial strain. Or she may be exhibiting the worst traits of an introverted or sensitive personality. Her prickly rejection can become a crucial moment for you to affirm to her that you understand her pain and to confirm your unshakable commitment to a relationship with her. Consider the following dos and don'ts the next time your daughter says, "Mom, just leave me alone!"

Don't Walk on Eggshells

The natural mistake mothers make (especially hover mothers or moms who mother from beneath) when our daughters become surly or withdrawn is to tiptoe around them, hoping the bad mood will just go away. When we walk on eggshells around our moody teenagers, we send them the message that they are dangerous, too much for us to handle. They already feel like ticking time bombs, and our anxious accommodations confirm that we're not the ones to turn to in the midst of an impending explosion.

When your daughter is mean or hurtful to you, don't act as if nothing happened. You might wince and say, "Ow, that hurt." Practice honest, nondefensive responses to your daughter's verbal assaults:

- "Wow, you must have had a really bad day."
- "Your words sting, but I'll give you some space."
- "A lot of people must have been mean to you today, because you don't usually act this mean."

Your daughter may continue to lash out at you or withdraw from you, but your acknowledgment of her words tells her that you hear her and you're not going anywhere. When you let her know that her mean words sting, you always provide a platform from which she can apologize later. I am not suggesting that you listen to a barrage of insults or abusive words. You may need to stop the interaction with the promise of reconnection later. You might say something like, "Stop. You are hurting my feelings. Let's talk about this after dinner." You can let her know the impact of her words, that you are stronger than her cruel words, that you can and will stop the conversation, and that you will be there when she can communicate without venom.

Don't Take It Personally

You will have to remind yourself of this often and pray without ceasing! Even when your daughter's words seem personal and even if she insults you directly, her words rarely have anything to do with you. Her cruelty and rejection come in part from all the pain and pressure she has experienced in relationships. Even if your daughter's mean-spirited words are simply a result of her not getting her way and she is lashing out at you, don't take it personally! Becoming personally entangled in her mood of the moment puts you right in the middle of *her* territory—a land mine–infested quagmire. When you take your daughter's words personally, you are tempted to defend yourself, and then you will not be effective in guiding her toward emotional maturity.

If you are in a particularly tempestuous time with your daughter, write these words on sticky notes and place the notes on your bedroom mirror, the dashboard in your car, and the sink in your bathroom: *Don't take it personally.* If you don't take it personally, you will be able to love your daughter and listen to her—even when she is pushing you away.

Do Ask What You Can Do

The Bible tells a story of relational aggression between a mother and daughter-in-law—only this time the mother-in-law was the one pushing away.

After both Ruth and Naomi lost their husbands, Ruth asked her mother-in-law if she could travel with her to Bethlehem. Naomi responded, "It is more bitter for me than for you.… Look…your sister-in-law is going back to her people and her gods. Go back with her" (Ruth 1:13,15, NIV). Naomi was saying, "Just leave me alone!"

Ruth's response to Naomi challenges me in relationships that feel cruel and confusing: "Let me go to the fields and pick up the leftover grain behind anyone in whose eyes I find favor" (Ruth 2:2). Ruth offered to give of herself in spite of her loved one's rebuff.

When your daughter is mean and spiteful to you, can you offer her kindness? Are you afraid that if you are kind you'll be teaching her to treat you badly? Remember, first acknowledge the mean or hurtful words, and then offer her the nourishment of kindness. I'm afraid we've distorted "tough love" to mean that *we* must become tough and withhold our love. Jesus described a different kind of love:

> I'm telling you to love your enemies. [How much more your daughters?] Let them bring out the best in you, not the worst. When someone gives you a hard time, respond with the energies of prayer, for then you are working out of your true selves, your God-created selves. This is what God does. He gives his best—the sun to warm and the rain to nourish—to everyone, regardless: the good and bad, the nice and nasty. (Matthew 5:44-45)

Practice offering the kind of startling "give your best" kindness that God offers, regardless of how your children behave. Instead of being reciprocally nasty to your hostile daughter, try saying: "It sounds like you want to be alone. Can I bring you something to eat or drink?" or "I can't imagine how bad your day must have been. Is there anything you'd like me to do for you tonight?"

When you do reconnect, don't hide the impact of her hurtful words or actions. Offer empathy if you can connect her mood to her circumstances, and give her the chance to try again—both to express herself and to experience your interest and support.

I am writing this during Kristin's first week of her senior year of high school. I have this plan to take pictures of every event and document every-thing that happens during this last year of school. On the first day I was wait-ing to take Kristin's picture at breakfast, getting into her car, and driving off to school. After the first picture, Kristin snapped at me, "Mom, I don't have time for this! This is stupid. I don't know what the big deal is! It's just another school year!"

After she left, I dissolved into tears, crying about my hurt feelings because of Kristin's response to my "big idea" and because it *is* a big deal to *me* that this is her last year of high school. After the first box of tissues, it dawned on me that Kristin's gruffness might have been a defense against an unarticulated jumble of emotions about being a senior. I know that girls this age sometimes "act out" to defend against the anxiety of growing up and leaving home. I also know that Kristin can be just downright unpleasant in the morning, so a photo shoot was probably not a good idea.

When Kristin came home I said, "I know that in the mornings you don't have a lot of time for extra stuff, so I can understand why my picture taking was annoying. But your response hurt my feelings. This year is a big deal for me, and I want to remember it—for both of us. Please don't make fun of me or be mad when I try to take pictures or do something else to memorialize this year. And I promise I won't ask too much of you in the mornings."

Kristin rolled her eyes. "Okay, Mom. Just don't make too big of a deal about it!"

Yeah, right.

DO GIVE SPACE AND INVITE RECONNECTION

When your daughter asks you to leave her alone, give her space. Honor her demand, but always return with an invitation. Your invitation conveys the message, "No matter what you do or how ugly you behave, I will always love you and be your mother. I will never exclude you. You always have a place of belonging with me." *Meet your daughter's relational aggression with relational commitment.*

Once again Jesus models this toughest and most tenacious love when He offers an invitation to those who have distanced themselves from Him: "Here I am! I stand at the door and knock. If anyone hears my voice and opens the door, I will come in and eat with him, and he with me" (Revelation 3:20, NIV).

Practice inviting reconnection with statements like these:

- "I'll give you some space, but can we eat breakfast together tomorrow?"
- "I hope you can have some quality time alone, but this weekend let's go shopping."
- "I bet you have a good reason for being so mad. I'm going to check back with you in an hour to see if you feel like talking."

HONORING PRIVACY AND TEACHING SELF-REGARD

By the time Kristin was five years old, she already had a strong spirit and expressed it passionately. Her response after being scolded one day reminds me of the confusing tendency we have to hurt ourselves when we are in pain. She looked me right in the eyes and declared, "Fine. I'll just go to my room and cut off my nose!" Her five-year-old sentiments echoed the adage, "She cut off her nose to spite her face."

When our daughters shout, "Just leave me alone," and stomp off to their rooms, they are vulnerable to being tempted to withdraw in pain and inflict further hurt upon themselves. Psychologists describe this phenomenon of self-harm as "acting in." When adolescent boys are confused and hurting, they often act out by getting into fights, driving fast and recklessly, or participating in outlandish pranks. Girls are more likely to act in—starting strange eating behaviors, beginning to mutilate themselves, or withdrawing in depression. Our daughters' protests to be left alone can become a pathway to darkness and destruction, or they can be an invitation for us to encourage healthy privacy and self-regard.

---

*Men and women…feel similar types of pain, but they often express it
in different ways. There are many ways to explain why women
hurt themselves more often than men do…. Men act out.
Women act out by acting in.*

—DUSTY MILLER, *Women Who Hurt Themselves*

As your daughter enters puberty and embarks on the journey into adolescence, she needs more privacy. The following dos and don'ts will help you evaluate what you are teaching your daughter about personal privacy and dignity.

Don't Use Your Daughter's Room as a Place of Punishment

When we ground our children in their rooms, we are sending the message that their rooms are a place of punishment rather than retreat. Encourage your daughter to spend time in her room when she is tired, angry, or distressed in order to rest, reflect, and rejuvenate herself. I am convinced that one of the reasons girls lock themselves in their rooms and inflict self-harm is that they have been banished to their rooms in punishment. Girls simply continue the punishment—often to unthinkable extremes.

Don't Invade Your Daughter's Privacy Without a Really Good Reason

Make your daughter's room a privacy zone where she can play the music she wants, talk to her friends on the telephone, and be sure that others will not enter without first gaining permission. The only reason I support for reading your daughter's diary or searching through her things is if she has completely shut down and you cannot communicate with her at all. If you suspect that drugs are in her room, or evidence of other destructive behaviors, tell her you are going to search her room and would like her to be present as you look.

If you find contraband, confront the behavior but confirm to her that you want her room to be a safe place of retreat and that one of the reasons you have searched her room is to keep it safe. I know that practicing this principle is tricky. What are you supposed to say if you find birth-control pills, drugs, or other scary artifacts? One mother I know gives us a great example.

She suspected something was wrong with her daughter for a number of reasons and searched her daughter's room for clues. She found a home pregnancy test. Perhaps you can imagine the looks on both mother's and daughter's faces when Mom pulled the kit from a cubbyhole in the closet. She wisely said, "I don't think we should talk about this right now. Let's both think about it and talk tomorrow over breakfast. Let's go to that place you like—The Egg & I."

This courageous mom called a few friends and asked for their advice, and she "prayed without sleeping" (the mother's version of 1 Thessalonians 5:17).

Over breakfast she said to her daughter, "I just want to know what's going on. I won't be mad. I'm sorry you've had to keep something so important secret."

Her daughter, not surprisingly, was defensive, "It doesn't mean anything, Mom. Give me a break."

Her mom pressed on. "I suspect that it means you've had sex or thought about it. It probably means that you've wondered if you are pregnant. I remember the first pregnancy test I took..." She told a funny story about a pregnancy scare after she was first married. She didn't worry about explaining the differences in their situation or lecturing about sex outside of marriage. She offered a bridge of connection, hoping that if her daughter crossed over, she would have the opportunity to offer substantive support and direction.

Her daughter took a step that opened the door to a hard and important conversation. "I'm sorry, Mom," she said, her voice beginning to crack. "I've never been so freaked out in all my life."

Do Help Your Daughter Create a "Sacred Space" in Her Room

Give your daughter free rein in decorating and arranging her space. Encourage her to make it special and make it hers—with candles, pictures of friends, mementos of her life, and so on. You may wince at a poster she chooses or a decorating scheme (or lack of one) she picks, but let her choose.

One mother I know prides herself on her beautifully decorated home. She picked out designer paint, curtains, and a matching bedspread for her teenage daughter's room, and she wonders why her daughter doesn't spend any time in it. Her daughter wanted clutter and funky decorations. She spends more time at her friends' houses than in her clean, tastefully decorated room.

Do Continue to Practice Giving Space and Reconnecting

When your daughter shouts, "Just leave me alone!" practice responding, "Yes, I will give you space. I want you to have the time you need in your room. Feel free to play the music you enjoy as loud as you want. I'll let you know when it's time for dinner."

Are you afraid? Afraid she'll be out of control? Afraid the neighbors might hear her music and call the police? I can almost guarantee you that they won't, and it's even likely that the loud music won't last very long. Your daughter is testing you. Out-of-control adolescents almost always develop in response to a power struggle. Do you trust your daughter to make her own choices? Maybe you don't—fully. But what better place for her to experiment with choices than in her own home? Invest in a really good pair of earplugs!

Developing Authentic Power

Most girls and their mothers develop a pattern of relating that takes on a life of its own in the midst of emotional turmoil. Interactions become a little dance that is soon so familiar that mother and daughter can even sense when it is about to begin. And yet they seem helpless to stop it once it starts.

Don't Dance with a Moody Daughter

Perhaps your daughter comes home from school in a bad mood. The dance begins. You start to walk on eggshells around her because you don't want her mood to get worse. Your daughter takes advantage of your tiptoeing and stomps on everyone's feelings. Your home becomes tenser as the dance goes into full swing. You confront your daughter or attempt to soothe her mood, and she lashes out at you, "Mom, just leave me alone!" You may go after her or let her go, but her statement makes it clear that she is taking the lead in this dance. You may respond by pestering, withdrawing, or attempting to force your daughter to participate in family life, but the pattern of relating remains set: She is acting, and you are reacting.

This dance is really about power, and what your daughter learns about personal power during these interactions can impact her relationships for the rest of her life. Your reactions to her threats and demands can easily give her the message that the way to be powerful in relationships is to distance herself or become demanding. If your daughter feels stronger or superior when she lashes out and withdraws from you, she may be deceived into thinking that strength is gained by cutting oneself off from others. If you walk on eggshells around her, she will feel the false power of gaining an upper hand in relationships. If you try to pressure her to be with you and talk to you, she may hold on to her power to distance herself from you and drive a wedge between the two of you.

Cindy and her daughter, Cami, came into counseling because they were both tired of the destructive dance they were doing with each other. Cindy began by telling me about Cami's sullen, disrespectful behavior. "She just needs to learn how to control herself," Cindy lamented. I could feel embarrassed agitation almost seep from Cami's pores while her mother told on her daughter.

"Where did you learn to talk like that?" I asked Cami.

Without missing a beat she answered, "From my mother. You should hear her and my dad fight. They yell and swear—I hate it." A tear trickled down Cami's cheek.

Now it was Cindy's turn to be embarrassed. I said quietly, "Sounds like you both need to learn what to do when you're angry or hurt."

It's painful to acknowledge when we have modeled emotional immaturity to our daughters. Often our daughters' moodiness is a reflection of our own. Cindy began the hard work of growing herself up so that she could guide her daughter toward emotional maturity. I asked her to spend a week observing her daughter's moody expressions and think of them as a mirror reflecting her own words and actions.

Cindy came back the following week with a repentant heart and a fervent desire to seek my help for herself first, and then for her daughter. She humbly admitted, "My bad temper and difficult marriage have been fertile ground for Cami's angry and disrespectful attitudes."

The good news is that if one person stops participating in the unhealthy pattern of relating, the dance stops. You want to teach your daughter that true personal power comes from being connected to others through listening, vulnerability, kindness, patience, persistence, and commitment. When you sense that the old familiar dance is about to begin with your daughter, take time to stop, remind yourself of who you want to be in the relationship, and do something different. Practice the hand-in-hand mothering style described earlier. Be intentional about offering your daughter the opportunity to develop personal power.

Do Become a Detective to Understand Your Daughter's Moods

Lauren and her mom, Jill, came to see me for counseling when Lauren was a freshman in high school. Her grades had begun to drop from As and Bs to Cs and one D. Lauren became moody around her family and often withdrew to her room. She also started painting her fingernails black. Her mother had seen one poem Lauren had written that was about loneliness and alienation, and even hinted at suicide. Her mom was understandably scared. Jill and her husband grounded Lauren until she could raise her grades, and they called me for help with her emotional turmoil.

Lauren described to me a sadly typical experience in her first year of high school. She wanted to belong but felt overwhelmed by the sheer number of other students and the maze of social rules for belonging. Lauren found friendship with a few others girls who also felt awkward and confused in the new social setting. Lauren and her new friends bonded over shared loneliness and feeling outcast. They introduced one another to music and fashion styles that reflected their moods. They commiserated together about parents who didn't understand and just wanted them to make good grades in algebra and geography.

During this same time a few kids in Lauren's geography class began to tease her about her physical development. As often happens, the teasing took on a life of its own when these high-school bullies discovered that Lauren was an easy target. She turned red and didn't talk back. Lauren started to ditch geography rather than face the taunting about her large breasts. She didn't tell her parents or teachers because she didn't want further embarrassment or alienation. Lauren was trapped in high-school hell.

When Lauren's parents grounded her for her poor grades, Lauren retreated to her room—not to study algebra but to anguish over her life. She hated it. She felt powerless over peers and the cruel and unusual rites of passage of high-school life. Her parents unwittingly diminished her power even further by banishing her to her room. Her room became the breeding ground for despair. Lauren resented her parents and clung to the only power she felt she had: She shut herself off from them even more.

The first thing I did with Lauren in counseling was ask her to bring some of her writings to share with me. As I read of her anger and anguish, I looked for the "light" in her expression. Often it was only in a word or a hint of emotion, but I commented not only on her pain but on her yearning to belong, her desire to be understood, and her sense of justice. I asked Lauren's parents to relax their restrictions. We negotiated an arrangement that if Lauren would keep up with her assignments during the week, she could spend time with friends on the weekend. The last thing a depressed teenager needs is to be restricted from social interaction.

It took a while for Lauren to trust me enough to tell me about the harassment at school. I wanted to call the administration and personally hurt and humiliate the perpetrators, but I understand the way high school works. Lauren and I told her parents first about the bullying. I helped her parents understand that Lauren's moodiness at home was a clue to the relational pain she was experiencing at school. I asked her parents to practice offering kindness and connection at home as well as enforcing a moratorium on all teasing from Lauren's siblings. Then we worked with Lauren on new responses to the harassment. Lauren gathered the courage and self-regard to say, "Cut it out," and learned to turn away with her head held a little higher rather than freezing in shame.

I encouraged Lauren to continue expressing herself through her fashion choices and nail color. I coached her parents to recognize that this expression was a form of personal power and that to condemn it or forbid it would result in a power struggle with Lauren that they would lose. I understand that it can be scary for parents to see their children wearing dark colors. If your daughter experiments with black nail polish and wears only dark-colored clothing, look for the "light." Compliment her on her attention to personal hygiene, her declaration of independence from the Barbie-doll style of some high-school girls, and her creativity in finding her own style. When parents relax, this power struggle often diminishes. And if it doesn't, I promise that your daughter won't be wearing black nail polish and safety pins along the seams of her pants when she's forty!

Surviving is important. Thriving is elegant.

—Maya Angelou

I noticed from Lauren's diary entries that she had a sense of "word design," and I encouraged her to join the yearbook staff. Once again some high-school savvy comes in handy. School groups like yearbook, band, and foreign language clubs are often places for more socially hesitant kids to connect. These groups are not magnets for the popular kids who can also be exclusive in their social interactions. Lauren did join the yearbook staff and began to make friends there and feel a part of her school.

Lauren had also been doing research on breast reduction surgery. When she first talked to me about this surgery, I suggested that she ask her mom if she could consult with her pediatrician. Lauren was so informed about the surgery and so aware of her own personal experience that she became her own best advocate. Her pediatrician referred her to a plastic surgeon, and the surgery was scheduled for the summer after her freshman year.

Although Lauren's body-altering actions may seem a bit extreme, it is a wonderful illustration of the development of personal power. I wish more parents would understand the extreme circumstances their children often confront in high school and respond with extreme compassion and creative choices.

Just for the Two of You

Ask your daughter if she sees bullying or harassment at school. Ask her how she thinks adults should respond. Listen for clues about her experience.

Try the exercise I suggested Cindy try with Cami. Observe your daughter's moodiness. Have you ever had any outbursts similar to hers? When? Do you fight with your husband? Are any of your expressions similar to what your daughter says to you?

Ask your daughter what she would like to change in her life. Is it possible to implement some of these changes? Remember that developing personal power is far more important than following all the rules. For example, can you give your daughter permission to take a "ditch day" from school once a semester? Go shopping. Watch movies together. Let her create a break from the rigors of high-school life.

Ask yourself, If I could do anything for my daughter, what would it be? Now evaluate if together you can enact some of the changes and opportunities your heart dreamed of.

Be on the lookout together for emotionally mature women who use their power to reveal their unique giftedness for purposes greater than themselves. Take note of women who make changes, help others, and creatively express themselves.

Lauren was able to become vulnerable about her emotions and experiences. As she told her parents about her experience and how she felt, they relaxed restrictions and supported her in healthy personal change. Lauren began to take note of her unique abilities and found an outlet for her talents and self-expression. Finally, she learned that although she felt pain, loneliness, and injustice, those things did not have to extinguish her compassion, her connection with others, and her ability to make positive choices.

The following is a poem Lauren wrote for her mother after completing her freshman year (quoted with Lauren's permission). I don't know about you, but I think her words are far more important than straight As on a report card.

> You have loved me, you have cared.
> Outside the madness a bond has formed that we share.
> Together we've been through life in hell, and hell on earth,
> But through it you've shown me how much I'm worth.
> If I had this year to live again I would not change a thing,
> Because our honest to God bond has been worth everything.

Chapter 7

"Mom, I'm So Stressed Out!"

The teen's world reflects the adult's world, only it is more intense, dramatic, extreme,
and less restrained than the broader society in which we all live.

—Patricia Evans, *Teen Torment*

Anxiety. Most teenage girls wake up with it and go to sleep with it more days than not. Many adolescents can't perform in school, become isolated and withdrawn, or experience physical aches and pains because of it. An increasing number of teenagers are medicating it with alcohol and drugs. And some teenage girls become so paralyzed by it that they cannot function in daily life.

Eleven million Americans suffer from anxiety disorders during the best of times, and with the constant barrage of news about war, terrorism, and economic instability these days, our "privileged nation is feeling unusually vulnerable and uncharacteristically anxious."[1] Mix the national epidemic of anxiety with normal adolescent stress, and we have a generation of teenagers who are living on the edge.

In 2003 counselors were reporting a six-fold increase in the number of teenagers seeking help for anxiety-related problems.[2] I have seen a similar pattern in my own counseling practice. In fact, I have found anxiety to be the common thread that links the many reasons why teenagers come to counseling. Depression, withdrawal, acting in, and eating disorders—all can be traced to a root of anxiety.

Anxiety does not always manifest itself in extreme behaviors. Anxiety exists on a continuum that can be manifested in panic attacks or social paralysis, but it can also be reflected in the everyday experience of typical teenage life. Perhaps you've seen a version of the following scenario acted out in your house:

"Lisa, I need you to take out the trash before we leave for school."

"I can't do it right now, Mom. I can't find anything to wear, and I have this huge zit right in the middle of my forehead."

"Lisa, it's almost time for school. You should have thought about what you were going to wear last night." *Lisa's mom looks at her watch in exasperation.*

"I didn't have time last night. I had that chemistry homework to do, remember?" *The panic is starting to rise in Lisa's voice.*

"I seem to remember that you were on the telephone all night last night. Now hurry up. Get ready to go. And take out that trash." *Lisa's mom begins to gather her briefcase and purse in preparation to leave the house, her anxiety on the rise as well.*

"Mom, I was talking to Alyssa last night. Her parents are fighting and she's afraid they're going to get a divorce and she had a really bad day at school. One of the guys in our biology class started to…"

Lisa's mom cuts her off. "I don't have time to hear it right now. We have to go."

"Mom, I'm so stressed out! Really, everything I put on makes me look huge, and no matter what I do, this zit gets bigger and bigger. I know I'm going to fail my chemistry test today. I tried to do the homework, but our teacher just doesn't explain it very well. If I don't do well, I won't be able to play on the basketball team. And something is really weird with Alyssa. I know that she has a lot going on, but I feel like she is always ditching me to be with someone else. Mom, I feel like I'm going to explode! Can you please call me in to be late this morning? I'm too stressed to go to school!"

The anxiety in Lisa's voice is matched by the anxiety in her mother's voice. "I can't call you in to be late. I can't be late to work. I've got a big presentation today. Just find something to wear and get ready to go. *I'll* take out the trash!"

THE ANATOMY OF ANXIETY

Lisa's feeling that she is going to explode is rooted in some biological realities. Understanding the anatomy of anxiety is a gift that we can give our daughters. I am particularly passionate about the need to be informed and aware of anxiety because of my own experience with it. I had my first panic attack when I was nineteen years old. I felt as if my heart was going to explode out of my chest, I felt tingles up and down my spine, my palms were sweating, and I was terrified. I thought I was going crazy. Over twenty years ago doctors did not know what they do today about anxiety, and I was told by a well-meaning doctor that I was nervous and stressed out. It wasn't until more than ten years later that I learned there were biological and chemical reasons for my mounting anxiety and that there were specific steps I could take to manage my stress.

Although most girls will not suffer panic attacks or experience anxiety in the manner I did, all teenage girls and many preadolescent girls experience some anxiety.

WHAT IF...
I break a bone?
I can't use the phone?
I get stung by 100 bees?
I blow out both of my knees?
I can't play soccer?
My books fall out of my locker?
I live on the streets?
I have to eat beets?
I get cancer?
I fall with my dancer?
The bogeyman jumps out of my closet?
My mom loses her check deposit?
My parents get divorced?
I die falling off a horse?
I do bad in school?
I drown in a swimming pool?
My parents forget me?
A robber gets me?[3]

—Kristin Hersh, sixth grade

Since teenage life is lived on an intensified scale, stress is an part of the adolescent experience. It's important for us to r when we look at our schedules, budgets, and tasks, our daughters' lives might seem stress-free compared to ours. But to them, their lives are extremely stressful. Even at low levels, anxiety causes muscle tension, vulnerability to illness, and impaired judgment.[4] When we help our daughters understand what is happening in their bodies and their brains, we equip them to use anxiety to develop the muscles of emotional maturity.

The brain was designed by God to respond to stressors automatically. When the brain perceives a threat—be it from a potential terrorist or uninvited acne—it triggers a chemical response within milliseconds. Anxiety causes the brain to produce a hormone called CRF (cotropin-releasing fac-

JUST FOR THE TWO OF YOU

The following exercises are intended to help you and your daughter increase your awareness and confirm your understanding of anxiety.

The first step in combating anxiety is identifying it. If your daughter feels stressed out a lot, keep a calendar that rates her anxiety level every day on a scale of 1 to 10. Make a note if something specific happened that day to intensify her anxiety (such as a test at school or conflict at home) or if she did something unusual that might have diminished her anxiety (such as some form of recreation). Be sure to notice how her monthly hormonal cycle affects anxiety.

Keep in mind that headaches, stomachaches, sleeplessness, and rapid heartbeat can all be symptoms of anxiety. As you help your daughter become self-aware, confront anxiety head on by naming it. Make it a practice to say, "I am feeling anxious." Naming anxiety can keep it from going __rground and getting ahold of us when we are unaware.

__ a list of possible stress-provoking situations. Use the following
__ is stressful to your daughter:

__ to come over to your home
__ with a classmate

unavoidable
member that

tor), which signals the pituitary and adrenal glands to flood the bloodstream with adrenaline, norepinephrine, and cortisol. These stress hormones direct the body's resources (all of its organs and systems) to either fight or flee the stressor. Our bodies and brains were intended to regroup after a stressful event and rest. Ideally, the "door" that releases the stress hormones is supposed to shut. Scientists are discovering, however, that in our fast-paced, stress-laden culture, many people do not experience enough "downtime" to let their bodies and brains rest. The result is that the door in the brain stays ajar and allows stress hormones to continue being released.

Furthermore, some people's brains are "rewired" (as a result of illness,

- giving a speech
- talking on the telephone to a friend
- expressing a personal opinion about a movie or book
- ordering food in a restaurant
- playing sports or participating in gym class
- eating or drinking in front of others

For each event, discuss the biological cycle that takes place: (1) the stressor, (2) release of stress hormones, (3) action, and (4) rest. Talk with your daughter about how this process might go awry. For example, freezing instead of talking or developing physical symptoms like a headache.

When I was in the sixth grade, I distinctly remember the anxiety I felt when I had to give a speech in class. Rather than talk about it and develop ways to deal with the stress, I began to scrape the sides of my thumbs with my nails. I scraped so intently that my thumbs bled. This became a habit for me that took years to break. I didn't understand until much later that stress goes somewhere in the body. Rather than becoming aware of it and dealing with it in healthy ways, I allowed it to pop out in a destructive habit.

Look for stories in the news of the "fight or flight" response at work—a heroic escape, a dramatic rescue, or remarkable athletic accomplishments. Take note of the amazing automatic response of the brain and its impact on the body.

trauma, or other experiences) so that the release of stress hormones is contin-uous, resulting in chronic anxiety and other anxiety disorders. Adolescents are especially vulnerable to anxiety, and the stress hormones are more likely to have a significant effect on their still-developing brains. Dr. Bruce Perry of the Child Trauma Academy explains, "Kids learn everything faster than adults. If they have the stress response on a lot, their bodies say, 'I'm in a world where I need to use these systems a lot.'"[5]

[Adrenaline] is the key stress hormone in our bodies. It was designed to be used only in emergencies, but we are now all so stressed out that we literally live one continuous emergency lifestyle!

—ARCHIBALD HART, *Adrenaline and Stress*

Understanding our biology is important for two reasons. First, it makes sense of our physical and emotional realities. As we take our daughters' emo-tional experiences seriously, we give them a sense of security when we say, "There's a reason why you are feeling this way." Second, it can lead us to tools that can help us manage anxiety. We give our daughters a sense of empower-ment when we say, "There are some things you can do when you are feeling anxious that will help you feel better." We will examine these tools later in this chapter.

THE COMMUNICATION OF ANXIETY

I confess to being a worrier. I worry that my son won't graduate from high school when he gets a C on a test or that he won't be able to hold down a job be-cause he never makes his bed. I worry that my daughter won't think seriously about life because she is a cheerleader or that she'll marry an irresponsible man because her date to the prom brought her home fifteen minutes after curfew. Worrying is part of the job description of being a mother. We can't turn off the impulse any more than we can will ourselves to stop blinking.

When Kristin was in first grade, her class made plans to have a "bike hike." When Kristin brought the note home from school detailing the event, I announced that "we" had better get busy learning to ride a bike without training wheels. "We" started practicing immediately. I coached and ran after Kristin while she pedaled, tumbled off her bicycle, and bravely got up to try again.

After about an hour of practice, Kristin was tired and wanted to take a break. I anxiously urged her on. "Do you want to be the only one in your class who can't ride a bicycle without training wheels?" Kristin took a few more tries on the bike and finally spoke to me with wisdom beyond her years. "Why do I have to keep practicing because *you* don't want to be the only mother in the class with a daughter who can't ride a bicycle without training wheels?"

Of course, not all our worrying is as irrational or self-absorbed as my worrying about Kristin's bicycle skills. We live in a time of painful and heart-stopping experiences—some without happy endings. One of the most significant challenges of mothering is to get a grip on our anxiety so that we can authentically and powerfully guide our daughters toward emotional maturity. When we are drowning in our own worry, we cannot be the life preservers for our daughters that we are intended to be.

There is an inverse relationship between the intensity of worrying and the capacity for creative problem solving.

—HARRIET LERNER, *The Mother Dance*

When our hearts and minds are filled with worry, we communicate anxiety to our daughters. And when our primary communication is worry, we can't make known other things, such as compassion, curiosity, good judgment, and spiritual values. Practically speaking, worrying doesn't change anything, and it keeps us from more essential matters of mothering. Sometimes our anxiety has been passed down to us from our own mothers, and it's easy to get our own unresolved issues all mixed up with our daughters'. Those things that are unspoken or unresolved from our own past will become entangled with our worries about our daughters.

For example, my mother was a champion worrier, and I must admit that I gave her a few things to worry about. My adolescent exploits fueled my mom's anxiety, and her worry fueled her suspicions about me. I lived with a sense that my mom always thought I was up to no good. Rather than confront specific behaviors head on, deal with them, and move on, we lived with a pervasive sense of foreboding that kept us feeling we were against each other. We never learned how to resolve specific incidents, so the misdeeds of the past fueled worry about the future.

When my own children entered adolescence I felt a growing sense of depression. I couldn't name it and didn't realize that it was connected to my experiences with my own mother until I caught Kristin in a lie. I discovered that she had lied to me about going to a specific movie. She confessed her lie on her own, we talked about the consequence of some lost trust, and we ended the conversation with a hug. I didn't realize the lost trust had lingered until later.

Just for You

Make a list of all the things you worry about with regard to your daughter. Considering your list, reflect on your own adolescence. Is your anxiety about your daughter rooted in your own adolescent experiences? Answer the following questions:

- Did my mother worry about similar things with me?
- How did I respond to my mother's anxiety?
- How do I wish my mother had responded to me?
- Is my worry right now primarily about my needs or my daughter's?
- Am I making assumptions about my daughter when I worry?
- Is my anxiety intensified because I feel out of control?

Ask your daughter if she thinks you are a worrier. If she says yes, ask how you communicate worry. Reflect on your own mother's parenting style. Are there similarities?

Recall the times your mother believed in you and expressed confidence. How did you feel and respond? Now recall the times when your mom did not believe in you and expressed anxiety or fear. How did her state of mind affect you?

I suspect that even today, if your mother is living, her opinion of you still matters. Reflect on how your mom expresses worry about you or confidence in you today. How does it affect you? What do you wish your mom would say about you or to you today?

A few weeks passed, and Kristin asked to go to another movie. I agreed that she could go, and we confirmed the specific movie and times. But I felt restless and resentful while she was gone. When she got home, I didn't ask her much about the movie, and she noticed. "Mom, what is up with you? I feel like you've been mad at me ever since I asked to go to the movies. Don't you want me to have fun?"

As I examined my own feelings, it dawned on me that I was afraid of letting my daughter have fun. I was afraid that she would betray my trust again, grow away from me, and end up in an entrenched battle of suspicion as my mother and I had. My reaction to Kristin's experiences was rooted in my own experience with my mother, and I was setting myself up for difficulties we weren't even having!

I have discovered that many mothers dread adolescence and anticipate disconnection from their teenage daughters, just as I did. Now would be a good time for you to reflect on your own past experiences and examine whether they are revving up your anxiety with your daughter. Resist the temptation to skip over this time to think about yourself. I understand that the laundry is calling, but taking time to focus on your own anxiety and its impact on your relationship with your daughter can keep it from swallowing up the relationship and will protect your daughter from absorbing your anxiety. Anxiety is, after all, contagious.

COMMUNICATING CLEARLY

Whenever you find yourself worrying about your daughter, try the following steps to clear anxiety from the communication channels and keep wisdom and love flowing:

1. Recognize how your daughter feels. Envision your anxiety as a parade that wants to pull your attention from your daughter. Catch yourself falling in line with this parade of frightful characters, and step out of that line. Focus on your daughter and the whole array of signals she is sending that give clues to her frame of mind and state of heart.

2. Think and pray about what your daughter needs. During times of crisis, conflict, or challenge, you can easily become so absorbed in what you need that you don't see what your daughter needs, much as I did in the bike-riding episode. Anxiety can result in your becoming almost like a sleepwalker in your daughter's life, stumbling over interactions and mumbling meaningless words. Ask yourself, Since my daughter is feeling _____, what does she need from me right now?

3. Recognize what you can and cannot give your daughter. As you recognize your daughter's feelings and needs apart from your own, you will become aware of what you can and cannot give her. If she needs comfort, you can offer her solace. If she needs advice, you can give direction. If she wants everyone to like her, you can offer her your own love and assurance, but you cannot control her world of friendships. If she wants her divorcing parents to get back together, you can assure her of your presence in her life, but you can't promise a restored marriage. It's important for mothers to accept what we cannot control. We do little to soothe our daughters' anxieties when we promise what we don't have the power to deliver.

You won't be able to encourage your daughter to express emotions
in healthy ways if your own emotional life is suppressed, distorted,
or out of control. Before we examine how to help our daughters with
their emotions, take some time to courageously peer inward at
your own emotional life.

—SHARON HERSH, *"Mom, I Feel Fat!"*

---

4. Accept feedback. Give the message that you are curious, compassionate, and available, but that you will also give your daughter space. One of the greatest gifts you can give your daughter is the assurance that she can come and go. When you are attuned to your daughter's body language or verbal signals indicating that she needs a hug or a break, you give her the assurance that she can fully express every aspect of her wild and unpredictable personality, knowing that you will remain a calm and connected presence.

THE GIFT OF ANXIETY

Did you read the heading of this section more than once? It is not a typographical error. Anxiety is inevitable; it is part of the experiences of mothering and adolescence. But anxiety can be a gift—a gift that can draw us closer in relationship to our daughters, our daughters in relationship to us, and each of us in relationship to God. Every emotion tells us something important. Anxiety is no different. Anxiety is a gift because it tells us to be vigilant, to rest, and to trust God.

Be Vigilant

"Finally, brothers, whatever is true, whatever is noble, whatever is right, whatever is pure, whatever is lovely, whatever is admirable—if anything is excellent or praiseworthy—think about such things" (Philippians 4:8, NIV). The apostle Paul outlined the "parade" we are to follow with our thought lives. Anxiety diminishes when we are vigilant to "take captive every thought to make it obedient to Christ" (2 Corinthians 10:5, NIV). We don't have to preach a sermon to our daughters to banish anxiety. We can model for them and guide them toward emotional maturity by practicing vigilance.

1. Affirm that thoughts are real. Based on your understanding of biology, you can remind your daughter that when she has a thought, her brain releases chemicals in a millisecond that affect her body.

2. Encourage your daughter to be aware of how her thoughts affect her.

Just for the Two of You

Develop a routine with your daughter in which you challenge negative thinking. The key to vigilance is not in denying or dismissing what your daughter is feeling but in answering it. Below are some "points of challenge" that you and your daughter can watch for:

- saying "always," "never," or "everyone"
- focusing on the negative (Negative realities exist, but they don't deserve our sole attention.)
- predicting the future (One experience does not guarantee another.)
- reading someone else's thoughts ("I know she hates me.")
- being defined by your feelings ("I feel stupid." "I feel like you will never trust me.")
- guilty words ("I should be friends with everyone." "I ought to get straight As.")
- taking things personally ("My friend didn't talk to me this morning. She must be mad at me.")

Remind your daughter that when she is angry, sad, jealous, happy, excited, or anxious, her body responds. Thoughts matter!

3. Remind your daughter that feelings of anxiety don't always tell the truth. Partner with your daughter in the lifelong quest of discerning when anxiety is telling the truth or not. Sometimes our intuition tells us to be afraid and watch out, and it is warning us of some future harm. Sometimes our anxiety tells us that we can't do something or that we're stupid. If we never challenge these thoughts, we accept them as true, and they impact our behavior.

4. Encourage your daughter to talk back to her anxiety. We can train our thoughts to be positive and hopeful. As you encourage your daughter to express herself, you become her ally in challenging her negative thinking. When your daughter says, "I can't do anything right!" you can tell her, "I know you feel that way right now because you didn't do well on your test at school. Those negative feelings are swirling around in your body right now. Doing poorly on a test does not mean that you are a bad person." When we think a negative thought without challenging it, our mind and body react to it. We have the amazing opportunity to become partners with our daughters in taking away the power of negative thinking.

REST

Anxiety is often a signal that we need rest. When our brains are flooded with adrenaline and our bodies respond, eventually we become depleted. We were designed to need time for restoration and recovery. God gives a beginning instruction to mankind: "Six days thou shalt work, but on the seventh day thou shalt rest" (Exodus 34:21, KJV). Rest is vital for our bodies, souls, and spirits. Anxiety is a gift because it reminds us to rest. If we don't, our adrenal glands become overactive in order to meet the continual demand, and the self-destructive side effects of chronic anxiety continue unabated.

Once again we have the opportunity to model something to our daughters: rest, which is an integral component in emotional maturity. When you are feeling anxious, remember that your daughter will believe in the importance of rest and restoration in proportion to what *you* believe and model in your life.

Evaluate your activities. Have you just completed a major task or gone through a challenging experience? Your anxiety may be telling you that you need a break.

Welcome the letdown. Don't be afraid to lie around for a day or take some time for yourself. (We recently took a "vacation" to Disney World. I could not help but think about the sensory overload in that environment and how counterproductive it is to our rest and recovery. Our culture does not promote a healthy picture of vacation.) Make sure you encourage your daughter after exams, sporting activities, or social events to rest before she plunges headfirst into the adrenaline-producing events of adolescent life.

Pamper yourselves. Schedule naps, a bubble bath, or an easy, fun conversation over hot chocolate and cookies.

Schedule a massage. Touch is critical for healing, rest, and restoration. According to George Howe Colt and Anne Hollister, among the numerous benefits of massage is that it "lowers anxiety in depressed adolescents."[6] Many cities have massage therapy schools that offer massage by students at a significantly reduced cost.

Find a kind of exercise you enjoy doing together or separately. Exercise releases endorphins that induce a sense of well-being and combat anxiety. Participate in exercise not as a punishment for being fat but as a means of increasing blood flow, which nourishes the brain so that it can function properly. I know that many moms are confronted with resistance when they suggest their daughters exercise. Offer an incentive to your daughter based on your passionate belief that physical exercise is a matter of life or death for your daughter's body and soul. Offer a trade-off: television time for a walk around the block. Suggest a humorous reward: You'll give up your morning coffee (ouch!) if she'll take an aerobics or Pilates class at the gym.

Trust God

Entire books have been written and eloquent sermons have been preached about trusting God. I do not presume to have new insights or radical information when it comes to this subject. I know that I am prone to anxiety and wander away frequently from my own trust in God.

One of the things that spike my anxiety intensely is car problems. I feel powerless to figure out the problem and fix it. Recently the brakes on my Jeep began to make a dreadful noise. I took it to the repair shop and waited with growing anxiety for a call back. When the call finally came, I took the news hard. The mechanic explained all the details of the repair, which I immediately forgot when he told me the cost! I got off the telephone and started to cry.

With the hysteria only a woman understands, I explained to my daughter that the cost was high and we didn't have the money, and I went on to talk about overdrawn checking accounts, outstanding bills, and the looming costs of college for my daughter. My anxiety was contagious, and in the midst of this nonsensical conversation about brakes and college, my daughter exclaimed, "Mom, call that guy back and tell him he's got to lower his bill. *My future depends on him!*"

Her conclusion brought me up short. Anxiety grows in proportion to our reliance on false resources. I want my daughter to know that her future is not dependent on the popular girls at school, her grade in geography, her ability to wear size 2 jeans, or Mom's current bank account balance. She will know this to the degree that *I* know *my* future is not dependent on a large bank account, clean closets, or brakes on my car that never give out. Our future (past and present, too!) rest in the One who said, "Fear not, for I have redeemed you; I have called you by your name; you are Mine. When you pass through the waters, I will be with you, and through the rivers, they will not overwhelm you. When you walk through the fire, you will not be burned or scorched, nor will the flame kindle upon you.... Because you are precious in My sight and honored, and because I love you" (Isaiah 43:1-2,4, AMP).

My friend Stacie and her daughter, Katie, had a lot to be anxious about. Their family had recently been split apart by a divorce. They had just moved to a new town, and Katie had started high school in a new school where she didn't know anyone. Katie began complaining that she couldn't sleep at night. She said that she couldn't turn off her brain. Her sleeplessness caused other problems: irritability, fatigue, fear of future sleepless nights. Anxiety was not only robbing Katie of sleep, it was also stealing the possibility for a good start to her freshman year of high school.

Fortunately, Stacie understood anxiety. She explained to her daughter about anxiety and all of its possible ramifications. She told Katie, "It makes sense that you are anxious. You've been through a lot and are in the midst of exciting and challenging changes." She suggested that she and Katie develop a bedtime ritual to confront the nighttime anxiety head on. They began their ritual with music (Katie's choice) on the CD player and a few lit candles. They fixed steamers (flavored warm milk) and sat on Katie's bed and sipped their drinks. Katie summarized her day, and her mom prayed for her. Sometimes Stacie would give Katie a back rub. Katie drifted off to sleep with the candle burning. Stacie would come in later and blow out the candle and pray for her daughter one more time. Stacie and Katie wove vigilance, rest, and trust into a nightly ritual that calmed Katie's anxious heart and mind and cemented their relationship.

Katie is twenty years old now, and she still calls her mother occasionally at bedtime and says, "Light a candle for me, Mom. I need your prayers." Stacie lights a candle, prays for her daughter, and, as she blows out the candle, gives thanks that even the swirling storms of anxiety can lead us to seek out one another and depend on God.

Chapter 8

"Mom, Everyone Hates Me!"

Your daughter's friendships with other girls are a double-edged sword—they're key to surviving adolescence, yet they can be the biggest threat to her survival as well.

—ROSALIND WISEMAN, *Queen Bees and Wannabes*

Sarah's parents were going through a divorce—a messy divorce. Sarah had been in the middle of a custody battle and had seen more bad behavior by adults than any child should have to experience. When Sarah came to me for counseling, I expected to hear about her parents' custody fight and any one of a number of aspects of this chaotic divorce. But she began her first session by saying, "I am having a lot of problems with my friends. There's this guy I like, but he doesn't know it, and I don't know if I should tell him, and it will probably get all weird if I do. And more important, my best friend since second grade has a boyfriend, and she is with him all the time, and when she's not, she talks about him, and she doesn't seem to care about me at all anymore. And I don't know, sometimes I feel like *everyone* hates me!"

Although I have read about it in sociology and psychology texts and have seen it in the lives of my own teenagers, it still surprises me when I hear about the overriding importance of friendships to adolescent girls. Sarah's focus on her friendships was probably, in part, a distraction and defense against the pain in her family situation, but her concerns about friends were also the real focus of her life at this time. There are two foundational realities about teenage girls and their peers that parents need to understand if we hope to help our daughters as they navigate the emotional turmoil of their relational worlds: (1) our daughters were designed for relationship, and (2) our daughters' relationships with peers feel like the most significant relationships in their lives.

A Definite Design

The first reality is that we were all created for relationships. Your daughter's diary entries about friends—girls and boys—and her hours on e-mail or the telephone reflect her design for connection. At no time in your daughter's life has she been more aware of her desire for relationships than now. Her design is revealed in her focus on friends and in the simple reality that only girls go to the restroom in pairs!

Just as your daughter's emotional development is awakening to her desire for friendships, she enters a social world of rules and conduct that is sometimes cruel and always confusing. She experiences a profound longing for relationship in the context of a hierarchy of cliques, popularity, geeks, and losers.

Just for You

1. Recall some of your earlier experiences in relationships—a game on the playground, a Friday night slumber party, a date to the homecoming dance. What did these experiences tell you about your desire for relationships?
2. What do you think about, pray about, dream about *most* today? Are relationships central in your experiences and desires?
3. How do you view your own desire for relationships? Pitiful? A beautiful reflection of God's design? Weak? Wise? Your heart for your daughter and her relationships will be a reflection of how you see yourself in relationships.
4. How would your relationship with your daughter change if you honored and even saw as "holy" her intense desire for friendships?

A Dramatic Reality

The second reality is that during their teen years, girls view their relationships with their friends as the most important relationships in their lives. They experience intense connections, loyalty, and heartbreak during these tumultuous times in which they have banded together. These intense connections can confuse parents, make mothers feel passed over or left out, or tempt parents to dismiss the significance of these relationships as merely part of "teenage drama."

Kristin came home from high school one afternoon and slammed her book bag to the kitchen floor. "How was your day?" I asked tentatively.

"Horrible," she yelled, "and I don't want to talk about it!"

I was caught in a familiar dilemma. Do I run after her and risk disconnection by invading her space? Do I ignore her mood and risk disconnection in my distancing? Do I remind her of our fun plans for the weekend and risk disconnection by dismissing her pain of the moment? Do I lecture her about her attitude and risk disconnection by placing myself above her struggle? Or do I tell her that I'm sure God will work everything out if she just trusts Him and risk disconnection by spiritualizing the situation?

Deep within us is a desire for fulfilling relationships so intense that even the daily or disappointing realities of life cannot extinguish it. What else could motivate women to buy more than fifty million romance novels each year, to turn "chick flicks" into blockbuster movies, and to talk for hours on end to each other about relationships.... An undeniable longing beckons us, urges us, haunts us, and reminds us that we were designed to experience rich, deep, passionate, and mutual relationships.

—Sharon A. Hersh, *Bravehearts*

When you think about it, all of the responses that come naturally and make sense in the midst of our daughters' emotional angst are potentially disconnecting. But I know better (so I thought), and so I prayerfully and intentionally approached my daughter with a connecting response. I asked God for help and approached Kristin with a compassionate intention to ask if there was anything I could do for her.

As I knocked on her bedroom door, I felt compassion flood my heart. I was prepared to ask really good questions. But before a single word came out of my mouth, Kristin let me have it: "Mom, didn't you hear me? I don't want to talk to *you*. I had the worst day of my life. Stephanie and I are fighting.

Derek [Kristin's boyfriend at the time] is going to break up with me. My whole world is falling apart, and you are only making it worse!"

Kristin and I have a good relationship. Her hurtful, harsh, and unjustified words were unusual but not completely foreign to our interactions. I knew she must have had a really bad day. But in that moment I was crushed. I was unfairly accused and immediately felt defensive. I forgot about connecting habits or compassionate attention. I launched into my best martyr-mother speech. "I work all day to take care of you. I go out of my way to make sure you have a great life, and this is the thanks I get?"

Kristin's heart did not melt at my attempt to take her on a guilt trip. She just raised her voice a few decibels. "I never asked you to do anything. Just forget about it. Nothing matters anyway. I hate my life!"

Oh how I wish I could tell you I got off this train that was clearly headed for disaster, but I pressed on. "Fine. You can just take care of yourself from now on. See how much you like that life!"

Clearly I don't always practice what I preach. But I hope you'll join me in the profoundly simple acknowledgment that mothering a teenage girl is hard, and none of us does it right all the time. There's something about our daughters' emotional turmoil that pushes our buttons of defensiveness. I went to my room after my enlightening conversation with Kristin, prayed for a few minutes, did some deep breathing, and turned on *Oprah* to see if she had on a parenting expert who might be able to help me!

After a "time-out" from mothering, I slowly began to remember the foundations of this chapter: that my daughter was more keenly tuned in than ever to her longings in relationships, and that her friendships with her peers were the most important relationships in her life (making their sometimes hurtful and unreliable words and actions deeply wounding). It seems like a simple concept, but it is one I often forget in the context of mothering Kristin and wanting to become her ally in the midst of relational ups and downs. *Kristin's friendships are really important to her.* She might have known her friends for only a few months, and they might drift away from one another after high school, *but they are really important to her.* Her friends don't do her laundry or make her lunch, *but they are really important to her.* Her friends might hurt her or leave her out, *but they are really important to her.* I might not like her friends or understand their behavior, *but they are really important to her.*

When I force Kristin to choose me over her friends (this is true even in a conversation in which I try to pull her from her own concerns into my agenda) or to dismiss or ignore her relational experiences, she will choose her friends over me more often than not. Even if my intentions are to honor Kristin and her friends, when Kristin is hurt by her peers, I become an available "container" in which to dump her feelings just by showing up! Even more tricky is the reality that *I* set her up to choose against me when I criticize her friends, diminish her concerns, or play the martyr. The result is that she doesn't like herself (no child feels good about choosing against her

JUST FOR THE TWO OF YOU

The next time you have a conflict with your daughter, take a few moments to sort it out. First of all, identify everything you said and felt that was about yourself. Second, identify your daughter's feelings and needs. Ask yourself, What can I let go of that's about me? What specific need or feeling of my daughter can I address?

You might need to take some time to nurse your own hurt feelings or let your anger dissipate before you can clearly focus on your daughter. If you believe you need to address your daughter's disrespectful words, it is best to do this from a position of looking at yourself first. Most of us would rather fight with our daughters than face ourselves.

When you and your daughter are experiencing some "smooth water" in your relationship, ask her, "Apart from your family, who is most important in your life right now?" After your daughter has identified her significant relationships, ask some of the following questions to get a better glimpse of her relational world:

- "What do you like about your friends?"
- "What don't you like?"
- "If you were escaping a sinking ship and had to pick one or two friends to be in your lifeboat, who would you pick? Why?"
- "Which friend do you like to talk to when you're feeling down? Why?"
- "Which friend is most like you? most unlike you?"

mother), but she feels as if she doesn't have a choice. Remember, *her friends are really important to her.*

In my conversation with Kristin, instead of becoming her ally in developing friendships, I became the issue, unintentionally at first, and then actively as I took my own hurt from Kristin's words and hurled a few accusations back at her. This realization allowed me to go to Kristin and apologize. "I'm sorry I said some hurtful things that I didn't mean about your taking care of yourself and my threatening to stop mothering you, even though that's the furthest thing from my heart's desire. Will you please forgive me?"

My apology opened the door for Kristin to apologize as well. She also said, "When I say I don't want to talk about it, can you give me some time?" Point made and accepted.

I told Kristin I was available whenever she wanted to talk. Sometimes it can take hours (or days) for Kristin to want to go into the details about her complicated social world, but that day she opened up right away and talked about Stephanie, Derek, and many of the other realities of her relational life. I'm also aware that there are some parts of Kristin's social life that she doesn't tell me. One characteristic of a healthy mother of a growing adolescent is accepting that there are parts of your daughter's world that are hers alone.

A Distortion of Design

There are three potential distortions of our daughters' longings for significant relationships that can erode or harm their emotional development. Being aware of these potential distortions and being armed with strategies to help our daughters with relationships will teach them volumes about friendship, support, understanding, loyalty, and connection during this formative time. These distortions develop on a continuum, and although our daughters may not be characterized entirely by one distortion, they may be tempted to move in one of these three directions in response to the difficulties of relationships.

In this chapter we will focus on the more subtle distortions of relationship that occur in everyday adolescence and shape our daughters' relational lives. (We will look in part 3 at the more extreme forms of acting out or acting in that can come with each distortion.) The desire for friendships, the disappointments of relationships, and the drama of adolescence can result in a girl becoming a User, a Loner, or a Pleaser.

As is often the case with girls, my daughter has fallen into all three categories at different points in her adolescence. Her cries of "Mom, everyone hates me!" have become important occasions for her to look at her own relational skills and make changes. I realize that not all girls are willing to look inward; they just feel the hurt and disappointment from the outside. As moms, our responsibility is to honor our daughters' longings for friends and nudge them toward seeing their responsibilities in relational difficulties while we model healthy relationships for them.

Let's look at each of the common distortions of relationship and consider how we can be a true friend and help our daughters grow toward emotional maturity.

IS YOUR DAUGHTER A USER?

A User in the teenager world is a girl whose relationships are all about numbers and power. She uses friendships to boost her own status, which means that she can quickly discard friendships if they don't get her anywhere. Both boy and girl friendships are evaluated by appearance, popularity, and material possessions. Often friendship with one girl is designed to increase power by rejecting another girl. Friendships for a User are fleeting and may end over seemingly nothing. The depth of friendship in the teenage world is often challenged by the superficial realities of the adolescent culture, but a girl whose longings for relationships are distorted by becoming a User isn't interested in developing deep friendships. She just wants to acquire certain friendships to boost her sense of social and personal power.

A girl with this distortion of relationships is not necessarily a member of the most popular clique of girls in the school—this distortion can develop in any social group. A User does not just miss going deeper with her friends; she also deflects anyone from going deeper with her.

I uncovered this style of relating in one of Sarah's counseling sessions. I asked her, "How have your friends helped you with your parents' divorce?"

Much to my surprise, she responded, "Oh, they don't even know about it. They would think I was a loser if I complained about stuff at home. My friends are not about solving problems and having deep conversations, they're about parties and getting together and having fun."

"That sounds kind of lonely to me," I commented, "especially when you're going through hard times."

Sarah's answer revealed her distorted ideas about relationships. "My friends are there for me, but they don't really know me. They don't have to know me as long as they invite me to their parties."

Sarah got to the heart of the loss of being a User in relationships: superficial connection that will eventually fail to satisfy. A User never develops a real sense of self because she is too busy maintaining her image.

This would be a good time for you to reevaluate your own attitude toward relationships. Do you use them to prop up your own image? How many people really *know* you? Our daughters are often vulnerable to these distortions of relationship because they are imitating us or reacting to us. If your primary mothering style is mothering from above, your daughter may be particularly susceptible to this pitfall. She may suspect that you want her to follow your rules and advice to make you (instead of her) look good. Now is the time to participate in relationships for a sense of mutuality—give and take—for your own sake as well as your daughter's. If you believe you are vulnerable in this area, you may want to read something on developing healthy relationships (see the resources section on page 209).

I asked Sarah to consider talking with one friend about the more painful realities of her life. She came back the next week and told me how hard this disclosure was for her. "I don't want people to think I'm a loser," she explained.

I asked her to continue testing the waters for another week. The next time she came for counseling she said, "I told a friend about one of my parents' fights, and she told me she was afraid that her parents were getting a divorce too. I think we kind of helped each other." Sarah was taking the first steps in developing a true friendship.

I've often wondered how I got so trapped. What half-truths did I consume as a child? What lies? How did my desires go so awry? Perhaps there moved within me a hidden yearning to speak my... anger, wonder, sadness, and joy to another human being.

—Margaret Bullitt-Jonas, *Holy Hunger*

Kristin recently had a back-to-school party for several of her friends. During the party she asked if a few girls could spend the night. If you're a mother of teenagers, I know you can empathize with my heart-pounding confusion as I heard someone slip into our house at 2:30 in the morning! I turned on the hall light to see two of Kristin's overnight guests walking toward her bedroom. After a few questions I discerned that Kristin's friends had "used" spending the night with Kristin to sneak out and meet their boyfriends in the neighborhood.

Just for the Two of You

Teenagers tend to respond reactively or not respond at all when we tell them what to do. Instead, we can know and talk about people we respect. Keep a lookout for women and girls who model mutuality in relationships. Let your daughter see you ask your friends for help and support as well as see you come alongside your friends. Let your daughter see your joy in friendship as you experience both giving and receiving.

Teenage movies often tell the story of a User. Movies like *Never Been Kissed* or *Pretty in Pink* tell the stories of malevolent Users befriending outcasts in the school as a joke or part of a bet. If you notice that your daughter is starting to use friendships, you might suggest a movie night and watch one of these movies together. As you talk about the obvious cruelty and ugliness of the User in the film, you can pray that your daughter will recognize the appropriate moral and apply it to her own story.

Ask your daughter if she has ever felt as if you needed her to be a certain way for your own image. Apologize if it's appropriate, and be intentional about complimenting your daughter on her individual style and admiring her for her differences from you—even if you wince a bit inwardly about how she might look to your friends.

An important category for consideration as you evaluate your attitude about relationships is gossip. Gossip uses people in the worst way to destroy reputations and kill mutual honor and respect. If your daughter has heard you gossip about friends or, worse, gossip about her to your friends, apologize. Agree that you will support each other to stop gossiping.

The next morning after I fed the girls bagels, listened to them call their parents and tell them about their escapades, and sent them on their way, Kristin and I talked about the events of the night. I asked her why she'd let the girls "use" her, and she explained that they were girls whose friendship she had wanted all through high school. She thought this might signify a developing friendship. I asked her if they had given any other indication of wanting a friendship. She thought about it and shook her head.

I told Kristin that I understood sacrificing her own needs and self-respect to try to get people to like her. I told her that I was tempted to ignore her part in this midnight plan because I didn't want her to be mad at me, but that I respected myself too much as a responsible mother to do that. Kristin winced at the turn in this relational lesson as I told her she'd be staying home the following weekend.

Is Your Daughter a Loner?

As I reflect on all the adolescent girls I have counseled and am counseling, the most common impetus for parents to direct their daughters toward counseling is the fear that their daughters are withdrawing. Many girls have had painful experiences (teasing, sexual harassment, or the cruelty that can occur in everyday social life) in middle school or high school that have resulted in their withdrawal. Some girls feel inadequate to deal with the pressures of school life (due to personality type, social immaturity, or painful differences in appearance from the rigid teenage ideals), so they hang around on the periphery or isolate themselves at home.

If your daughter is a Loner, she may be an expert observer of high-school life. Sometimes she records her perceptive observations and painful realties in her journal or in poetry. I am surprised at how many girls tell me they write poems or stories and that their mothers have never asked to read them. Sometimes girls want to keep some of their writing to themselves, but often they want someone to read what they have written so they will feel known and understood. (The "Just for the Two of You" section that follows offers some suggestions to help you become your daughter's ally in relationships as she shares her writings with you.)

Just as with the User, it is important for mothers of girls who drift toward being a Loner to consider their own relationships. If you mother from a distance, your daughter may shy away from relationships because she feels uncomfortable with connection. Now is the time to examine your own distance and explain to your daughter your awkwardness or reluctance in relationships as well as your intentionality in developing friendships. If you've not worked on your own relational life, now is the time! If you need to find a

JUST FOR THE TWO OF YOU

Here are a few hints to help you with the challenging privilege and responsibility of helping your daughter:

1. Know your daughter's personality type. As you note various aspects of your daughter's personality, tell her stories of her childhood that confirm her personality type. You can tell your daughter that certain personalities are not always applauded in high school (being thoughtful, quiet, studious, etc.), but they translate well into real life. Tell her stories from your own experience or other people's experiences. For example, many therapists (myself included), artists, nurses, and ministers did not fit in during high school, but they thrive in the real world.

If your daughter does not fit in at school because of her values and beliefs, help her reframe her loneliness. I have a client who is mature beyond her years and holds fast to her convictions. She has only one close adolescent friend. I helped her identify that her loneliness is due to her values, not because she is repulsive or a loser. It soothes the pain a little for her to know that her adherence to principles and her distaste for some of the superficial and even disgusting behaviors of her peers is the reason for her aloneness. It's not because there is something wrong with her.

2. Ask your daughter if there is something that she is writing that she would like you to read. When you read her poetry or journal entries, resist the urge to comment first on what is troubling to you. Remember that writing is a healthy form of releasing emotions, confusion, and pain. This is another chance to develop your creative curiosity. Following are some helpful tips:

- Remember that for your daughter, disclosing her writing is equivalent to disclosing her heart. Compliment, affirm, and enjoy.

- Focus on a specific word and ask what that word means to your daughter.
- Ask why she picked this particular selection for you to read.
- If your daughter expresses negative thoughts or feelings, use the connecting habits from chapter 4 to respond to your daughter. For example, you might say, "It sounds like you were really angry that day. What did it feel like to put that anger on paper?"

3. Find groups and activities for your daughter to participate in outside the high-school world. If your daughter is in emotional turmoil, she may get stuck, and you may need to help her get moving again. Although you can't (and don't want to) do all of the work for your daughter, you can take some initial steps to help her out of her lethargy. Your daughter may resist if she's been hurt by relationships in adolescence or if she's an introvert. Here are some suggestions that you can prayerfully, persistently, and creatively present to your daughter:

- *Art as connection.* If your daughter is thoughtful or intuitive, help her find an art class or an art project in your church, her school, or your community center.
- *Service as connection.* Introverts are often compassionate because of their own loneliness. Find service projects or groups that need a hand. If your daughter likes older people, call the nursing home and ask about their needs. If your daughter likes babies and children, call the local crisis pregnancy center or a shelter for battered women to see if they need baby-sitters.
- *Social responsibility as connection.* I have discovered that many girls who tend toward being Loners are passionate about justice and social concerns. Learn about groups in your community that support social issues (homelessness, reading and literacy programs, etc.), and encourage your daughter to volunteer. You might need to volunteer with her to coax her along.
- *Faith as connection.* Encourage your daughter to participate in church youth activities or parachurch groups (InterVarsity, Young

(continued on the following page)

Life, Campus Crusade for Christ). Often if you mention to a youth leader that your daughter is shy or struggling with friendships, the leader will take your daughter under his or her wing.

Here are a few don'ts to keep in mind as you help your daughter.

- If your daughter has a different personality type from you, don't expect her to be like you. An introvert will not become an extrovert.
- Don't "arrange" relationships (have families over for dinner with girls or boys the same age as your daughter) unless your daughter is fully supportive.
- Don't force social situations (require your daughter to attend a school dance or activity). Encourage relationships in the context of interests or talents (as suggested above).
- Don't allow your daughter to sit at home every night watching television.

good book or class or seek counseling to help you overcome your reticence, do it. A rich relational life for yourself is a great gift to your daughter. Even if you've been a Loner for most of your life, I know that your heart for your daughter compels you to want something better for her. Use this longing to change yourself, and you will discover along the way that determining to model something different for her will bring rich rewards for you.

We have recently gone through some difficult and challenging days in our family. I found myself withdrawing and pulling away from relationships. As I recognized my isolation and reminded myself of my need for friends, especially when I feel depressed and am hurting, I became intentional about scheduling time with friends at least once a week.

After one engagement my daughter met me at the door when I came home. "How was your time with Traci?" Kristin asked.

"Really good," I answered.

"I'm *so* glad you did something with a friend," my daughter said.

"Why?" I asked, surprised by her enthusiasm.

"It just makes me feel happy to see you with friends," she answered.

I learned in that moment that my having friends lightens Kristin's burden of worry for me and also models for her the importance of friendship, especially when life is hard. Although teenagers are naturally self-absorbed and don't always pay that much attention to their moms' social lives, they can *feel* when their moms are supported. We have a clearer perspective on mothering and a lightness in our own emotional life when we are involved with others in satisfying ways.

The high-school social world is challenging for the most outgoing girls. If your daughter is naturally an introvert, she may decide to forgo a social life altogether because it's too hard. If your daughter has a strong sense of values and beliefs, she may avoid teenage social life because of the many temptations and foolish behaviors that teenagers engage in. As her mother, you want to affirm her personality type, respect her for holding to her values, *and* encourage her to be in relationships. This is a tricky task.

IS YOUR DAUGHTER A PLEASER?

Almost all females understand being a Pleaser. Our longing for relationship often leads us to ignore our own needs and preferences for the chance at a connection with others. Our daughters are no different than we are. Pleasing becomes a distortion of relationship and a potentially destructive style of relating when your daughter becomes willing to do almost anything in order to belong. Your daughter is a Pleaser if she values other girls' opinions, fashion styles, and values more than her own. She may even forgo developing herself because she is so busy adapting to others.

We must re-create an attractive and caring attitude in our homes
and in our worlds. If our children are to approve of themselves, they
must see that we approve of ourselves. If we persist in self-disrespect
and then ask our children to respect themselves, it is as if we break
all their bones and then insist that they win Olympic gold
medals for the hundred-yard dash. Outrageous.

—MAYA ANGELOU, *Wouldn't Take Nothing for My Journey Now*

I can recall when I was in middle school and met a girl who loved horseback riding. As soon as I met this girl, I knew that I wanted to be "in" with her. She exuded confidence and seemed to have an ease in social situations that I lacked. I told her, "Oh, I love to ride horses too. We should get together sometime." She agreed and invited me to ride with her the next weekend. Now the problem was that not only didn't I know how to ride, but I was also severely allergic to horses. I made excuses for that weekend invitation and the next two she offered, and then she stopped asking. We never became friends. I wonder what would have happened if I had tried to connect with her on the basis of my real interests instead of trying to accommodate hers.

A Pleaser will often become desperate to fit in, and that desperation can lead to bad choices and the erosion of personal values. She may dress to please

JUST FOR YOU

Do you know your style? Think about how you came to know what looked good on you, what you liked, and how you wanted to be in the world. Did your mother help you in this process? How? How would you have liked her to help?

Look through a photo album (include as many ages as possible). In which photos do you look like the authentic you?

Which of your friends know the real you? How do they encourage you?

I am a bit compulsive about time. I don't like to be late, and I like things to run according to schedule. One of my dear friends gave me a great gift when she said, "I love your quirkiness about time." Her simple sentence affirmed that she knew time mattered to me and that she accepts and loves me even if I am a bit uptight!

Now make some notes about your daughter's style. Look at photographs and remember her idiosyncrasies. Have you encouraged or suppressed her individual development?

Would you rather have someone describe your daughter as "a girl who can get along with anyone" or "a girl who knows what she wants and goes after it"? Why? What message are you sending to your daughter? What message would you like to send? Remember, a girl who won't say yes to her own preferences and desires probably won't say no to peer pressure.

the group, drink or smoke to fit in, or become sexually active to have a boyfriend. It's important for moms to know that when they discover these foolish choices, the root of them is not a "bad" girl, but a girl who is desperate to belong. This is a good time to evaluate your own relationships again. Our daughters sometimes observe a hover mother and believe that to be female they must forfeit their own needs and become consumed with satisfying others. Or perhaps you mother from beneath and model to your daughter that she isn't worthy of her own style, values, and opinions.

Is Your Daughter a Friend?

your daughter will experience cruelty from other girls. She he will gossip and be the victim of gossip. She will feel friends because they are jealous of her. She will feel nd there are days when she will feel as if she hates nan, cofounder of the Girls Empower program, mpted to tell her what to do and summarily ban- lled her heart."[1] Instead, you can model for her that we need friends, and that we must value e principles of hand-in-hand mothering that ity and self-respect so that when you observe your daughter drifti d being a User, a Loner, or a Pleaser, you can encourage her to become a friend.

I came into the kitchen one day last week to find Kristin hard at work on a poster. It was still summer vacation, and I wondered what she was working on so diligently. As I looked closer I saw several pictures pasted into a collage of Kristin and her friend Abby. A note beside the pictures read, "Abby, you are awesome!"

I asked Kristin about her motivation for making the poster. "Abby had a bad day yesterday. This guy she likes—John—just blew her off. She said she feels like she never gets the guys and no one ever wants her. I feel so bad for her, so I wanted to make this to cheer her up."

"You are such a good friend, Kristin. Abby is lucky to have you," I said.

Kristin's next words revealed to me that her longing for relationships and her relationship with me are guiding her toward relational maturity. "I know what it's like to feel like no one likes you. I know a note from a friend makes me feel so much better. Besides, I've seen you do so many nice things for people, Mom. I'm just doing what you taught me."

Now, that's awesome!

Your vision for your daughter's friendships will be a reflection of your own desire for relationships. As you model these qualities in relationships while your daughter is experiencing the adolescent social rites of passage, she will figure out who she wants to be. Of course, she may figure out relationships on her own. Many girls who don't have strong relationships with their mothers become wonderful friends. However, I can think of no greater joy than seeing our daughters grow into emotional maturity as they follow in our footsteps. The apostle Paul described the heart of a role model: "We simply wanted to provide an example...hoping it would prove contagious" (2 Thessalonians 3:9).

Just for the Two of You

The following is an exercise that can enable you and your daughter to connect over her longing for relationships and think through how she can be intentional in her friendships. "A [girl] that hath friends must shew [her]self friendly" (Proverbs 18:24, KJV).

Plan a special time with your daughter. Go for a manicure and pedicure. Take her to a bookstore that has a coffee shop. Go watch a girls' soccer game or tennis match. Pick something that is a reflection of your shared interests.

After your time together, find a quiet place to make an Absolute Yes! list. Explain to your daughter that friendships evolve over time and take some pretty hard hits. It's good for your daughter to have a reference point in relationships that she can return to when she's in danger of losing herself and all that she values. Here are a few ideas for your Absolute Yes! list to help get the two of you started:

- I will seek friendship with people I can trust.
- I will listen when my friends talk.
- I will try to stop gossip when I can.
- I will say "No!" when an idea or activity makes me uncomfortable.
- I will work on my girl friendships even when I have a boyfriend.
- I will pray for my friends.

Part III

Conquering Roadblocks to Relationship

One thing I've learned is that I'm not the mother I want to be when I sit, trembling, in the dark. Or pace on the dock, waiting for my daughter to come in one minute late so I can demand to smell her breath. I'm not the mother I want to be when I'm swirling out of control in a cyclone of fear. What is going to happen now? What if…what if…what if…what if… I don't want to live that way anymore. When I kneel by my bed and ask God to look after [my daughter] and trust that He is doing so, I'm choosing faith over fear. But I'm not just trusting her, I'm trusting Him. I am trusting Him with her.

—NICOLE JOHNSON, *Raising the Sail*

Chapter 9

Eating Disorders

Sometimes I feel all of this rushing and swirling spinning in my body and nothing can seep in.... Being this age feels insane at times.... I feel thick too and I don't like judging my body. I want to use it for exploring and dancing and living. I don't want to stare silently at its issues—but I do.

—Sabrina Ward Harrison, *Brave on the Rocks*

W e were eating dinner at Old Chicago," Debbie told me, as she and her daughter Reagan began their first counseling session regarding the event that brought them to me. I could tell that Reagan was uncomfortable. She looked as if she might either explode in anger or burst out in tears at any moment. "We all ordered our meals and were having a pretty normal meal out as a family," Debbie continued.

"You were already watching me," Reagan broke into the conversation. "You're always watching me—looking at me like you expect me to do something wrong all the time!"

"That's not true," Debbie said calmly. "I was wondering if you were going to excuse yourself to the bathroom like you've been doing a lot lately, so I was probably watching you a little more closely than usual."

Debbie directed her next words to me. "Reagan did eat over half of her meal and then excused herself to use the bathroom. I followed her. I waited for her to have enough time to get into the bathroom stall, and then I went into the bathroom. I could tell that she was throwing up."

"She followed me!" Reagan said with disgust. "I was going to the bathroom. That's private!"

"Reagan," her mom said quietly, "you were throwing up. This is serious. I had to know what was happening so that I could help you."

"It's none of your business!" Reagan shouted. "Why can't you just leave me alone?!"

Although throwing up is usually a private experience that no one wants to talk about, when a teenage girl uses throwing up to control her weight or deal with her body-image issues, it is a serious matter that needs to be brought into the open. In the mid-1980s, eating disorder specialist Mary Pipher wrote, "Bulimia is the epidemic of our time. Eight to 20 percent of all high school girls are bulimic."[1]

Throwing up is not the only behavior girls use to deal with eating, body-image, and self-esteem issues. Disordered eating can also take the form of binging, taking laxatives, starving, and exercising excessively. The most recent study by the Eating Disorders Awareness and Prevention Organization concluded that "*at least* forty percent of adolescent girls suffer from some form of disordered eating."[2]

An online poll conducted by Harris International in January 2003 found that the roots of struggles with body image and eating disorders begin early for girls. Seventeen percent of girls ages eight and nine and about one-third of girls ten to twelve thought they were fat and needed to diet. By the time they reach middle school, half of all girls will obsess about the flatness of their stomachs and the size of their thighs, and almost 40 percent will already have tried dieting.[3]

It may surprise you to learn that emotional turmoil at home, in school, or with friends is often the context in which body-image issues and eating disorders can be most powerfully addressed. In my book *"Mom, I Feel Fat!"* I explore in depth how moms can help their daughters develop normally and confront and conquer eating disorders. In this chapter we will look at a few preventive measures and intervention tools that will help moms deal with this serious and potentially life-threatening roadblock to their daughters' emotional maturity.

WHAT DO EMOTIONS HAVE TO DO WITH IT?

Body image has little to do with our actual physical body. Body image is the way we *see* our size and shape as well as how we *feel* about our bodies. As our growing daughters experience a broader and deeper range of what are often considered negative emotions—anger, jealously, disappointment, longing, hurt, fear, sadness—all of those feelings are often ascribed to the body. That is because the body is concrete; it is something we can see and try to understand. Its inevitable imperfections (accentuated by the glossy, unrealistic pictures of "perfection" in the media) are easy targets.

When life is stressful, it's easy to focus all our attention on one area we believe we can control—eating. Eating disorders develop when we fixate on eating and weight control. When life narrows down to cookies and fat-free yogurt or losing the next five pounds, it is a symptom of a potential eating disorder and an attempt to find control in an uncontrollable world.

—SHARON A. HERSH, *"Mom, I Feel Fat!"*

Just as body image has little to do with the actual physical body, eating sometimes has little to do with nutrition or even hunger. Eating is a form of expression and an important clue to what your daughter is feeling and needing. Eating (or not eating) is most often used to soothe emotional tension, control feelings of helplessness or inadequacy, and manage the emotions that can arise in the midst of life stressors such as beginning middle school or high school, trying out for a sport, breaking up with a boyfriend, or dealing with family problems. When any of these areas becomes magnified or distorted, your daughter may be at risk for an eating disorder.

One of the most precious gifts we can give our daughters is a positive view of their bodies *in the context of guiding them to emotional maturity.* How do we give this gift? Not all at once, but slowly, experience by experience, again and again. The volatile emotions of adolescence provide countless opportunities for you and your daughter to address body-image concerns and preempt the eating disorders that often result. Dr. Kathryn J. Zerbe, Vice President for Education and Research at the Menninger Clinics, describes this powerful link: "In summary, the struggle with body image faced by patients with eating disorders derives from their difficulty in expressing feelings and in developing a full emotional life."[4] Whether your daughter is ten or seventeen, you can become her ally now—and again and again—against an eating disorder by encouraging healthy emotional expression.

While working on *"Mom, I Feel Fat!"* I was surprised by the number of moms who expressed concern that even talking about body image and eating might give their daughters ideas for dangerous behaviors. My experience as a therapist of teenage girls strongly suggests that moms are wise if they gently begin to broach this subject before their daughters reach adolescence. The earlier onset of puberty in the twenty-first century, the media's bombardment of our daughters with images of sexualized and thin-looking girls, the inevitable roller coaster of emotions our growing daughters will experience,

Just for the Two of You

- Celebrate different emotions with your daughter—sadness after a good cry at a movie, laughter while watching the antics of a puppy, jealousy when a younger sibling gets attention, anger in response to injustice. Look together at these different emotions without fear or shame. Ask what each emotion can teach you, and discuss how it can turn into something constructive or destructive.

- When your daughter laments, "I feel fat!" ask what is going on in her emotional life. Take note that negative emotions are often felt as heaviness or weight in the body. To be truly healthy, we need access to our full menu of emotions and the freedom to express them.

- Look for opportunities to set aside time to ask your daughter how she is feeling about herself, family, friends, and school. As you are listening, don't look for "answers" to her emotions. Remind yourself, *She is really feeling this right now.* Care about what she cares about.

- Don't tease. Enforce a moratorium in your home on any teasing about body size or shape. Hurtful words can take on a life of their own in your daughter's mind and body.

- After your daughter has an emotional outburst, find a good time to talk about it. Ask her what she liked about your response to her and what she didn't. Ask her if she'd prefer to be left alone to sort things out during a hard emotional time, if she'd like you to simply sit with her, or if she wants you to talk her through it.

and the certainty that their peers are thinking and talking about body-image issues make it necessary to discuss the subject early.

When one of my clients was fifteen years old, she swallowed a whole bottle of Advil in hopes that it would make her throw up and help her lose weight. Westin ended up spending a night in the hospital due to the possibility of kidney damage from the Advil. When I went to visit her, the first words out of her mouth were, "I know I'm so stupid."

"I don't think you're stupid," I replied gently. "I do think you must be feeling some pretty intense emotions to make such a risky choice."

"I just hate my body," Westin said. "I feel so fat. I'm tried of feeling fat and never liking the way I look."

Westin's words were clues that her struggle with body image did not begin the day she took the Advil. She'd been *feeling* fat for a long time—probably since the onset of puberty, when, as her body began to change and grow, her emotional world similarly began to expand and intensify.

As you interact with your growing daughter about her changing body and swirling emotions, you don't want to overwhelm her, but your daughter's complaints about her body are excellent opportunities to probe her emotional life. If your daughter believes she has to "stuff" her emotions, then body-image distortions will take on a life of their own and may swallow her completely. Consider weaving the following questions into casual conversations with your daughter:

- Have you ever seen me stand in front of the mirror and complain about how I look?
- What do you think of my complaints? Have you ever done the same thing?
- Have you heard adults or friends talk about losing weight? Do you worry about your weight?
- Do you think you need to have a perfect appearance—just the right hairstyle, makeup, and clothes?
- Does perfectionism (or images in the media) make your body an easy target for self-criticism?
- Do you complain about your body more when you are tired, angry, lonely, or sad? Do you feel like you can talk about your emotions with your friends or with me?

- Who or what triggers painful feelings? Who or what triggers good feelings?
- What do others say about you that makes you feel bad or good?
- Does being around certain people make you want to lose weight?
- How does eating or not eating make you feel?

Don't be afraid to warn your daughter about the serious consequences of eating disorders. Read articles and watch movies about girls who have struggled with body-image issues or eating disorders. Be informed and open so that the wisdom and warnings about disordered eating are a natural part of your dialogue with your daughter—*before* eating disorders develop.

When I explained to Westin's mom, Gloria, about the roots of her daughter's body-image issues, she came up with a plan to bring this subject and her

Just for You

When our daughters begin to express concerns about and contempt for their bodies, it is time for us mothers to take a look—again—at how we feel about our own bodies if we are going to be authentic in guiding our daughters to healthy body images. Consider practicing some of the following activities yourself before inviting your daughter to do the same:

- Pull out photos of yourself at different ages. What photos are you drawn to? Why? When did you become aware of your body? When did you like your body? When did you not like your body? What was going on in your emotional life at these times?
- Become an expert on feminine growth and development. Create a library of resources that will assist you in understanding every stage of your daughter's growth.
- Evaluate your own care for your body. Is it fun, sensuous, and positive, or is it critical and negative? As you apply lotion, do you say, "This lotion smells and feels wonderful on my skin," or "I can't believe how old, wrinkled, and ugly my skin looks"?
- Write down all the ways your body serves you as well as all the things you could not do if you didn't have your body. Be thankful for it.

daughter's feelings out into the open in the context and safety of their relationship. She planned a weekend getaway for the two of them. They shopped, sat by the hotel pool, and talked. Gloria told Westin that she knew she had been going through a lot of changes and that it was normal to target the body as the scapegoat for all kinds of feelings. She asked Westin what she wanted to change about her body, and they came up with some strategies to tighten abs and tone other muscles. Gloria brought along some popular teen magazines, and they talked about the attractive images in the magazines and the unrealistic ones.

A recent study of more than three thousand fifth graders through eighth graders by researchers at the Medical University of South Carolina in Charleston found that one of the most influential factors for girls who struggle with eating disorders is their mother's relationship with food and body image!

—MARGERY D. ROSEN, "Is Your Child Headed for an Eating Disorder"

Most important, Westin and Gloria talked about feelings. Westin talked about wanting to fit in, fearing that she'd never be popular, and feeling awkward around boys. Her mom listened and told a few stories from her own adolescent years. When Westin and Gloria told me about their weekend, I congratulated mother and daughter for forming an alliance to challenge body-image questions, distortions, and concerns. I also reminded them that body-image issues will probably resurface as long as Westin's emotional climate continues to change.

EATING AND EMOTIONS

What if your daughter has started to dabble in strange eating behaviors or obsess about losing weight? What if you suspect that she might be skipping meals or taking laxatives? Now is not the time to abandon her to an "expert" and hang your head in shame at your perceived failures or inadequacies at mothering. It is never too late to become your daughter's ally in developing a healthy body image. You may need to consult with a therapist or physician who specializes in eating disorders, but *your* role is pivotal not only in helping your daughter overcome potentially dangerous eating behaviors but also in strengthening the bond between you as you guide her toward emotional maturity. Your daughter needs a good relationship with you now more than ever.

Eating disorders exist along a continuum. The most common time for the onset of an eating disorder is when a girl's body and life begin to change dramatically. Breasts as well as sexuality begin to bud, hips and an awareness of societal problems widen, and weight along with pressures and responsibilities begin to increase. We can help our daughters best at the beginning of the continuum by being aware and intervening proactively. *"Mom, I Feel Fat!"* describes more fully the continuum of eating disorders and the warning signs of anorexia, bulimia, and compulsive overeating. Following are a few warning signs and appropriate responses:

- If your daughter begins to skip meals or becomes secretive in her eating, don't ignore the behavior. Ask what's behind her not eating, and tell her that you want to know because you want to support her in healthy ways. After she explains her desire (usually to lose a few pounds), help her come up with a healthy strategy.
- If your daughter excuses herself to the bathroom after meals or leaves evidence of vomiting in the bathroom, don't ignore these signs. Tell your daughter you have noticed her behaviors, that you fear they are signs of an eating disorder, and that you will be finding help for both of you. Schedule an appointment with a counselor who specializes in eating disorders. This is one area in which you need to take charge. Don't take no for an answer from your daughter. Tell the therapist what you've observed, and let her help both of you deal productively with the problem.
- Even adolescent girls need to know that their mothers are stronger than they are. Our knowledge of the warning signs of an eating disorder and our strength in response to it might prevent the disorder from progressing further. Let your daughter know that she has control over her choice of food, but that when you observe her not choosing food at all or eating very little, you will intervene.
- Depression goes hand in hand with eating disorders. Experts debate

whether depression causes the disorder or the nutritional imbalance causes depression. Whatever the cause may be, you need to talk to your daughter about the risk of depression and educate both yourself and her about the debilitating consequences she is setting herself up for by depriving herself of necessary nutrients.

- If your daughter begins to eat only certain foods or very small portions at meals, or if she drinks water and diet drinks instead of eating, now is the time to talk about anorexia. Always begin any conversation by expressing a desire to understand what is going on in her life. Tell your daughter that you know she has a reason for her eating choices (or her choice not to eat). Help her articulate what she is hoping for, what she is afraid of, or what she is experiencing that justifies her unhealthy eating and exercise habits. Tell her you will support healthy choices and watch for unhealthy behavior. Once again, firmly tell your daughter that if you see repeated unhealthy eating behaviors, you will seek help for both of you.

- If your daughter is involved in a sport or activity that encourages weight loss (e.g., gymnastics, dance, ice skating), tell her, "When losing weight becomes more important than your love of the sport, you have to quit."

- Whenever your daughter puts herself down, challenge her negative mind-set. Encourage and compliment her and remind her of what is true.

- If you suspect that your daughter is compulsively reaching for food, help her identify the emotions she may be feeling. Stock your cupboards with a variety of wholesome foods. When your daughter reaches for a snack, ask:
  - Did something on television remind you of food?
  - Are you really thirsty instead of hungry?
  - Are you bored?
  - Are you avoiding doing homework or something else?
  - Are you stressed out about something?

Your daughter may roll her eyes at your questions, but you are attacking some of the possible roots of compulsive eating and are planting seeds for healthy choices to flourish.

Winning the Battle

Reagan and her mom had many difficult days ahead after Debbie brought Reagan's problem with bulimia out into the open. Reagan continued to deny that it was a problem, while her mom continued to watch for warning signs and tell me about them in counseling. Debbie's dogged determination not to allow her daughter to slip into an eating disorder without a fight paid off. Reagan wanted to end the conflict over her behaviors but discovered it was difficult to stop throwing up. She felt stressed about getting fat, and the only way she knew to relieve that stress was to purge. Her mom's faithful intervention eventually compelled Reagan to ask for help. Once Reagan was willing to admit that she had a problem and ask for help, she was on the road to recovery.

Reagan and her mom continued to meet with me on a weekly basis as well as check in with Reagan's physician once a month. The counseling not only helped Reagan and her mother understand the eating disorder and how to combat it, but it also cemented them as allies.

If your daughter is displaying signs of a possible eating disorder, and your informed, compassionate intervention does not nudge her away from the behavior, you will have to seek professional help. Find a counselor who specializes in adolescent eating issues as well as a physician who understands eating disorders. Remember that your daughter is not your enemy. If she is deeply entrenched in disordered eating, she may need hospitalization. It is almost impossible for a girl in the grip of an eating disorder to fight depression, develop self-esteem, and learn healthy ways of dealing with the pain and stress alone.

At no other time in her life will your daughter be hungrier for unconditional love. Even in the midst of this frightening struggle, treat her with respect and kindness. Your daughter needs to know that you are stronger than her eating disorder as you rely on God to be stronger. If you are not feeling strong, then do everything you can to arm yourself with information, take care of yourself, invite family and friends to support you in prayer (you don't need to tell them all of the details, but you can invite support while keeping your daughter's confidences), and relentlessly run to the truth that *God* is stronger than an eating disorder.

Now—and again and again and again—you can enter your daughter's world, connect with her, and engage with her about the tricky topics of body image and eating behaviors as you guide her toward emotional maturity. In a culture where your daughter is bombarded with skinny, glossy, and super-ficial female images, you can be a mirror that she can look into without fear as you reflect understanding, reassurance, wisdom, and love.

Cutting and Self-Injury

I used a safety pin to carve into my ankle, deep enough to draw blood....
I just wanted to change the way I was hurting. By making myself hurt
physically, I could make myself feel better emotionally.

—CHERISE WADE, "Skin Deep: A Story of Secret Cutting"

K aren tugged her sweater sleeves to cover her hands. I knew what she was hiding. And Karen knew that I would ask to see her arms. We had been meeting for therapy for about one month, and Karen's arms were evidence of the urgent matter that brought her to counseling.

About halfway through our session together, I asked Karen if I could see her arms. She unfolded her arms and pulled back her sleeves. Her left arm showed the scars of red welts she had carved into herself a few weeks earlier. Fading red lines traced from the center of her arm etched a pattern that looked like the rays of the sun a child might make in a much more innocent and less dangerous way. In the middle of the circle of scars a single word rose above the skin: UGLY.

Karen's right arm revealed an intricate design of lines and curves made by precise and delicate cuts of a razor into her skin. The scars on her arms had faded from the bright red of a few weeks earlier, but they still startled me with their jarring incongruity. I felt compelled to look at them the way I might feel drawn to stare at a horrific accident along the roadside. How did a girl think of such a thing? What internal emotional pain did such painful external etchings represent? What was Karen trying to say to herself, her parents, or to the world? What would happen next? Would she use a razor blade to harm herself more?

I had an idea of the answers to the questions that Karen's cutting raised in my mind because I had seen an alarming increase in the number of adolescent girls in my practice who were doing the same thing Karen was doing. But that did not keep me from feeling a pang of fear grab my heart. I could only imagine what the mother of a cutting daughter might feel.

Karen's mother, Kathryn, had discovered her daughter's secret cutting when she walked into Karen's room unannounced and saw her frantically grabbing clothing to cover her scars. Kathryn didn't even know what to call what she had seen on her daughter's arms. She didn't know who to talk to about it. Who would believe or understand or be able to help her help her daughter?

I saved Kathryn's message on my answering machine as evidence of her fierce love and courageous heart for her daughter. "I don't know what to call this," she began falteringly. "I think my daughter is using a knife or something to cut herself, but it's not just cuts. It's like a design carved into her arms. I don't know why she's doing this. I don't know what to do. Can you help us?"

Karen and I worked together for six months. She told me about the difficulties she was having finding her place in high school and about some troubles at home as well. Her father was a harsh man and often dismissed or demeaned her. During our work together in a safe place where Karen could talk about all that she was feeling, and with a watchful mom at home, Karen stopped cutting. Seven months into her therapy, Karen quit coming.

I called Karen's mom to ask why Karen wasn't coming to counseling. She explained, "Money is kind of tight, and Karen is doing so much better. She's not cutting anymore, so her father and I have decided that she doesn't need to come."

A few weeks ago I got a heartbreaking message from Karen on my answering machine. "I really miss talking to you," she said. "My parents say we can't afford for me to come. You probably can't call me and just talk. Oh well, I just wanted to say hi."

I did call Karen to talk for a few minutes and told her to call me anytime. Her story illustrates the roots of her extreme behavior—a depressive personality, an emotionally tense and unsupportive home environment, and parents with the wrong priorities.

Helping our daughters with scary emotional problems requires that we examine ourselves and our home environments and that we be willing to do whatever is necessary to sustain help and support.

Statistics About Self-Injury

Cutting is a painful secret that millions of people share. Experts estimate that between two and three million Americans are self-injurers. The SAFE (Self-Abuse Finally Ends) Alternative Program reports that 1,400 out of every 100,000 people in the general population have engaged in some form of self-injury.[1] According to SAFE founders Karen Conterio and Wendy Lader, authors of *Bodily Harm*, "The syndrome is more prevalent than most people think, and yet it is grossly underreported and misdiagnosed.... A particularly alarming aspect of the rising tide of self-injury is that the behavior is making its appearance earlier and earlier in the childhood and adolescent years."[2] In

Just for You

The concept of self-injury is probably not as foreign to you as you might think. The following questions are intended to help you gain insight into your own use of physical pain to relieve stress and begin to examine what you have conveyed to your daughter when you discovered that she was experimenting with using external marks to represent internal feelings. If you have conveyed shock or disgust in response to your daughter's behavior, you may need to apologize to her, recognizing that your self-righteousness was not rooted in honesty and understanding.

1. Did you bite your fingernails or scratch a mosquito bite until it bled? What made you stop? A lecture from someone else, stares from other people, self-regard?

2. Have you ever noticed your daughter biting her nails, picking at a wound, etc? How have your responded to her? With curiosity, self-disclosure (about your similar "bad habits"), disgust, or fear?

3. Has emotional tension ever resulted in physical pain for you? tense shoulders? leg cramps? a stiff neck? What did you do for the physical pain? How did you take care of the emotional tension?

4. Has your daughter experienced stomachaches or muscle tension when she is under strain emotionally? How have you responded to her? With a massage? With frustration?

fact, 90 percent of self-injurers begin the abuse during their teen years. Most cutters are female.[3]

Self-injury is the deliberate mutilation or marking of the body not with the intent to commit suicide, "*but as a way of managing emotions that seem too painful for words to express*"[4] (emphasis added). Self-injury can include cutting the skin, as in Karen's story, scratching the skin, or biting, burning, or hitting oneself. Many girls begin with scratching their skin and progress to cutting and burning because they discover they need to hurt themselves more severely or dramatically to get the same relief or "high" they got at the beginning of their experimentation with self-injury. Girls use razor blades, pocket knives, scissors, pieces of glass, and nails to cut themselves.

Girls' cutting can range from nicks in the skin to the carving of specific words or initials to elaborate designs. The cutting often comes after an emotionally tense interaction with parents or friends. It usually follows a pattern: The girl will go to her room, find her cutting implement, and sit quietly and contemplate the relief she believes self-injury will give her from the emotional angst. After the cuts are made, she will watch the bleeding and the formation of welts and scars on her skin. She may or may not bandage her cuts. She will most likely cut some place on her body that is not easily visible to others. Hiding the wounds is part of the experience of cutting. The pain-filled and secret world of emotional turmoil is the context for this unthinkable practice.

Following are some of the warning signs that indicate your daughter might be engaging in self-injury:

- She wears baggy, long-sleeved clothes all the time to hide injuries.
- She maintains a sense of secrecy—preoccupation, distance, furtiveness.
- She gives flimsy excuses for scratches or cuts.
- She has a stash of nails, pieces of glass, and razor blades.
- She withdraws socially.
- She makes self-contemptuous comments.

STORIES ABOUT SELF-INJURY

Karen's story is not unique among the stories from self-injurers. Her mixed message of "UGLY" on one arm and a beautiful design on the other revealed her confusion about her own sense of self in a mixed-up culture where appearance and image are all-important and yet rigidly defined.

Let me introduce you to a few more self-injurers. I want to tell their stories for two reasons. First, to encourage mothers that you are not alone. Your daughter's shocking and frightening behavior does not need to be a closely held, shameful secret. In fact, a secretive, ashamed response to your daughter's self-injuring will keep her in the grip of this behavior. Second, I tell these stories to plead your daughter's case. There is a reason she is injuring herself—a reason that if revealed and responded to wisely and compassionately can be a powerful clue to knowing your daughter and becoming her ally in developing emotional maturity. In the rest of this chapter we will examine the following three stories to learn about self-injurers and their families and to find the path to recovery for both of them.

Just for the Two of You

Perhaps it's time to gain a deeper understanding of your daughter's behavior. If you have discovered scars or designs carved in her skin or see evidence of cutting or burning, express to your daughter that you want to understand what's happening to her. Tell her that she won't be in trouble, that she will have a say in the course of action you choose, and that you want to understand her so that you can help her and love her better. Gently ask your daughter the following questions:

- Do you ever feel like you are drawn to cutting yourself—like a power is pushing you to do it?
- Do you feel relief or rest when you are done cutting?
- Do you think about cutting during school or at other times when you can't cut?
- Have you tried to stop?

If your daughter answers yes to these questions, she is in the grip of self-harming behavior and will need intervention in order to stop.

If you've discovered evidence of self-injury and your daughter won't talk to you, tell her that she will have to talk to a professional. Schedule an appointment with a counselor who understands self-injuring behavior in girls.

HOLLY

Holly came from a devoutly religious home. She attended church three times a week with her family. During her freshman year of high school, she changed dramatically. She began dressing in black clothes and wearing black nail polish and lipstick. She "bootlegged" forbidden music and played it in secret in her room. She attended a club at school (The Gay/Straight Student Alliance) with two of her new friends. When her parents discovered her music and learned about the school club, they grounded her for the rest of the semester (more than two months). Holly began a ritual of harsh self-injury. She burned herself regularly with matches or candles and did not hide the burns. Her parents observed them on her hands and legs, and even on her stomach. They were beside themselves with worry, anger, and shame and asked me whether Holly might need an exorcism.

MARINA

Marina's sister had been diagnosed with Sensory Integration Disorder (sometimes referred to as autism) when she was one year old, and Marina's parents had focused their full attention on Marina's sister and her needs. Marina's form of self-injury is described by experts as "delicate self-injury." It is a light cutting of the skin in an artful design. Her parents didn't know whether they should be concerned about Marina's cutting. They hoped it was a "fad" she would outgrow.

BLAIR

Blair's family was known in the community for their charity and volunteer work. Her mother was always impeccably dressed and loved to host extravagant parties. Blair was a little overweight when she started high school. By the end of her freshman year she was dressing in grungy, oversize clothes and had gained fifteen pounds. Blair started cutting on her legs, and her mother "freaked out" (Blair's words) when she discovered the word "fat" engraved on her daughter's thigh. Blair's mother wanted me to help her daughter lose weight.

GIRLS WHO SELF-INJURE

Girls who cut or otherwise injure themselves are as unique as their individual personalities. However, all girls who self-injure share two common perceptions: "I don't belong" and "I can't express myself." Understanding these two perceptions will not necessarily indicate the scope of an individual girl's struggle, but it can be a steppingstone to further understanding.

"I Don't Belong"

A sense of belonging is key to self-esteem and emotional maturity. A sense of belonging usually develops within family relationships and friendships, but it can be damaged a number of different ways. All three of the girls in the previous stories felt misplaced.

The damage to Holly's sense of belonging was probably the most difficult to detect. Holly's harsh self-injury indicated that she was angry with herself and those close to her. Her attachment to behaviors and groups that were far removed from her family also suggested to me that she had experienced a significant trauma.

After a few counseling sessions, Holly began to disclose to me an experience of sexual abuse during the summer before her freshman year of high school. The abuse had happened with a counselor at a Christian camp she had attended. She felt betrayed by Christians and decided she couldn't tell her parents because she was afraid they would think she was "bad." She told me that burning herself enabled her to feel that she was punishing herself for being "bad" and hurting her parents for not knowing what happened. This dual motivation explains why Holly didn't want to hide her injuries. It was an irrational plea for her parents to see that something had happened to her.

It's important to note that more than half of all self-injurers have suffered sexual or physical abuse during childhood.[5] If you know your daughter has been abused or suspect she might be hiding it, get as much help as you can from experts on sexual abuse. Sexual and physical abuse create a sense of shame in victims and a belief that they are "damaged goods." The profound loss of self-worth and belonging is so painful that perpetuating the injury against oneself makes sense. Girls who self-injure often say that they would rather hurt themselves than be hurt by someone else.

A loss of belonging may also stem from causes other than abuse. Marina felt displaced in her family because her parents' attention was focused on her sister. Blair felt out of place in her appearance-conscious family, and she felt out of place with her peers who were ruled by the stereotypes of "okayness" that dominate the adolescent culture. Of those who self-injure, 50 to 75 percent have an eating disorder.[6] As females grow up in our culture, they are bombarded with messages that encourage them to mold their bodies to fit the cultural ideal of thinness and sexuality. Self-injury is a statement of anger at self for not fitting in and anger at the world for imposing such unattainable and painful expectations.

Conterio and Lader succinctly articulate the emotional turmoil that results from not fitting in:

> If self-injury is a rite of passage, it is most certainly one designed to command maximum attention. It is at once a form of cultural affiliation with people who feel disenfranchised and "ugly," and at the same time a firm tweak at anyone who is supposed to care about the child.[7]

Girls who self-injure are also often experiencing turmoil at home that further fuels this sense of not belonging. A divorce or a depressed parent can create alienated relationships that leave a girl feeling alone. Teenagers who feel out of place often seek other "outcasts" through their music or friends (the way Holly did). Identifying with an outcast culture that dresses differently from the Ken and Barbie stereotypes and marking themselves with hieroglyphics of hurt sends the message, "I don't belong, and I am mad and sad about that."

It's important to note here that cutting is usually not a warning sign of impending suicide. The good news to parents is that cutting is a *way to sustain life*—a way of coping with hurt and rejection, relieving stress and anger, and gaining attention. Knowing that, my first advice to mothers is to begin to lavish attention on your daughter as if her life depends on it. Ask questions, find clues to her emotional state, compliment and comment—give the nourishment of attention to your emotionally starving daughter.

The questions in the "Just for the Two of You" section that follows may help you pay closer attention to your daughter's sense of belonging—or not belonging. Remember, these questions aren't intended to make you feel guilty or defensive; they are intended to help you see and understand your daughter's inner world.

JUST FOR THE TWO OF YOU

1. How did we pay attention to you when you were little? What do you wish we had noticed?
2. What group or groups do you belong to? What group or groups do you wish you belonged to?
3. Who notices you? Who do you wish noticed you?
4. What do you think people like about you? What do you think they dislike about you?
5. What groups do you hate? Why?
6. What group or groups do you think our family belongs to? Do you like or dislike them? Why?
7. What do you and I have in common? How are we different?
8. What things have happened to you that make you feel special? different? outcast?
9. What things have happened to our family that have made you feel lonely or different?
10. What do you wish could happen to change our family?

"I CAN'T EXPRESS MYSELF"

Expression is the regulator of the emotional life. When a girl can't express things because she is afraid or ashamed or prohibited, the emotion will simmer and boil and will eventually come out somewhere. *Self-injury is the expression of emotion.* Girls who cut themselves are expressing in slashes or incisions what they may not be able to express in words.

In the previous stories, all three girls felt that they could not express what they were feeling. Holly believed she couldn't talk about the sexual abuse because her parents would judge and condemn her, so she condemned herself and engaged in behaviors that would fulfill her malevolent prophecy about her parents. Marina believed her needs and feelings were not important to her parents compared to her sister's needs. Blair kept her feelings of self-contempt and rejection to herself, believing that her socialite mother would only condemn her further.

Listening to your daughter's emotional expressions may be hard and even painful for you, but learning to listen and empathize with your daughter is the necessary precursor to guiding her toward healthy self-expression and emotional maturity. In "Just for the Two of You" are some questions that will help you address your daughter's self-injury with curiosity and courage.

JUST FOR THE TWO OF YOU

1. When you cut, burn, or scratch yourself, do you think of it as a way of punishing yourself? For what?
2. Do you injure yourself to show others how bad you feel? What words would you use to express the same feelings?
3. When you cut yourself, do you feel like you are in control? What feels out of control?
4. Does the sight of blood or the scar from cutting or burning give you comfort? What feelings does it comfort?
5. Does cutting make you feel alive? What makes you feel numb or dead inside?
6. Does cutting keep your mind focused and help you not to think about so many things all the time?
7. Does self-injury help you relax? What things are you feeling stressed out about right now?
8. Do you feel bored when you cut? lonely?
9. Do you feel fat or ugly when you cut?
10. Do you feel angry when you cut? Can you tell me what you feel most angry about right now?

FAMILIES OF GIRLS WHO SELF-INJURE

Just as girls who self-injure share two common perceptions, families of girls who self-injure share two common characteristics. These characteristics are presented not to add to your sense of guilt as parents but to give you a sense of hope for what you do to help change the emotional climate of your family and your suffering daughter.

The stories of Holly, Marina, and Blair reveal the two characteristics that are common for families of girls who self-injure: the presence of loss (usually traumatic loss, such as a move, a family member's illness, parents' divorce, or even the death of a family member), and a rigid code of values that the daughter cannot incorporate into her life.

The Presence of Loss

The contexts for self-injury are numerous and complex, but woven throughout the many strands of each story is usually the presence of loss—the loss of childhood innocence, the loss of family structure, the loss of a friend or boyfriend, the loss of a long-held goal or dream.

In the previous stories, Holly's loss was violent and tragic: the loss of innocence, a sense of safety, and a feeling of control. Girls who self-injure say they experience a sense of physical calming after they cut themselves and feel as if they are more in control, even if their personal and family lives are out of control. Other girls talk about wanting to shock their parents or make them feel their pain.

Marina's loss was more subtle and yet more pervasive. She felt the loss of her parents' attention, interest, and participation in her life. Many girls who cut talk about feeling cut off from their parents because of their parents' busyness or preoccupation with their own problems. Many girls talk about hours spent alone in their rooms while their mothers are at work, their parents are watching television, or their parents are involved in their own social activities.

Just for You

Review the checklist on "life stressors" in the chapter on depression, and ask yourself the following questions:

- What has your daughter lost in the past year?
- How have you paid attention to her during the loss?
- What have you offered to replace what has been lost?
- How available have you been during this time?

If you feel that you have "flunked" this test, don't waste time condemning yourself. Your daughter needs you *now*. Take responsibility for your own preoccupation or skewed priorities and apologize. Find friends who will encourage you and hold you accountable to be more available for your daughter, or talk to a counselor.

I am not suggesting that we mothers don't deserve and need our own lives, but adolescence is a season in which our daughters need heaping doses of our attention, especially if they are experiencing losses.

Blair felt the loss of her little-girl body as she entered puberty. She felt cut off from the acceptable standard of her peers and her family. Her family's preoccupation with their image did not help Blair's sense of alienation. Self-injurers sometimes feel "cleansed" by their cutting, as though it rids them of all the "yucky" stuff inside that keeps them from feeling acceptable. A lack of affirmation and unconditional acceptance at home combined with the pretty horrific ups and downs of teenage social life can set up a situation in which a girl feels that she wants to cut herself, drain herself, rid herself of herself.

A RIGID CODE OF VALUES

A rigid code of values can be a list of rules that a girl has outgrown or a value system that seems hypocritical or too strict. It can also be a rigid standard of appearance with regard to weight, style of dress, makeup application, and so on. For Holly, her parents' religious beliefs held her hostage to the idea that the sexual abuse she had experienced made her "bad" and an outcast from her parents' faith. For those of us who hold clear values and beliefs, it is important that we don't use them to tear down other people. If our faith becomes a justification for criticizing and condemning others, it may become the excuse our daughters give for pulling away from us in fear of condemnation for their own foibles and failures.

Real religion, the kind that passes muster before God the Father, is
this: Reach out to the homeless and loveless in their plight.

—JAMES 1:27

Marina's parents had become so locked into caring for their special-needs daughter that they missed the special needs of Marina. Blair's family's social code and appearance-obsessed view of life left Blair feeling hopeless about ever being able to measure up. Remember that teenage girls grow up in an adolescent culture of rigid values about what it takes to be "in." When the teenage culture is combined with a rigid home environment—a home environment that makes no room for differences, that criticizes or mocks mistakes and failures, that condemns others—a girl can begin to feel as if there's no escape other than the private ritual of cutting herself behind closed doors.

Some girls who cut themselves are trying in destructive and counterproductive ways to separate themselves from their families to forge their own

Just for the Two of You

Following is a list of questions you can ask your daughter to see if she feels that she is unable to express herself to you. Don't by alarmed by her answers or try to debate them. Tell your daughter that you realize she is growing into adulthood and needs a context in which she can "try on" all her ideas and feelings.

Make a note of the answers that trouble you, and go back to them later to evaluate your distress. Do the differences between you and your daughter frighten or shock you? Are you afraid of where her ideas might lead her? How can you hold on to what you believe, listen to what she feels, and stay connected?

I know this sounds like a monumental task. I mean, what if your daughter wants to become a Hare Krishna, have sex, stay out all night, or skip the eleventh grade? One calming and helpful thought might be that the purpose of the conversation is not to convince your daughter she is wrong or crazy or to give her a short synopsis on all you hold dear. The purpose is simply to *stay connected*. Chances are if she discovers that she can't shock you or push you away, she will give up the idea of joining the circus. If you launch on a course to prove her wrong, you may inadvertently push her out the door.

Following are some of the questions you can ask your daughter:

1. Which family rules do you think you have outgrown?
2. What things about your faith are you questioning?
3. What three things do you value most right now?
4. What three things don't you care about as much as you used to?
5. Do you feel like you are more of an "artist" or a "scientist"?
6. What classes at school do you get something out of?

identities. Cutting becomes an unhealthy means of self-expression in place of healthy self-expression because a girl fears that the beliefs, likes and dislikes, fears and hopes she is forming will not be accepted by others. Sometimes a girl's forming of her identity by means of self-injury is a test to see if she can be different from her family and friends and still be accepted. When a girl

7. What classes do you wish you could drop?

8. Who are you mad at right now?

9. Who has hurt you or let you down?

10. When you are mad at me, how do you let me know?

11. Is it boring at our house? What would make our home more interesting?

12. What things about our family comfort you? If nothing does, how could we change that?

13. Do we show enough—or too much—affection in our family?

14. What do you think matters most to me? How do I show that?

15. Do you ever feel like the problems in our family are your fault?

16. Do you like the way our family appears? If not, why not?

17. Do you think we like the way you appear? If not, why not?

18. Do you ever feel like a burden? Why?

19. Do you ever feel like you want more attention?

20. Which of your thoughts and feelings do you think no one understands?

If you believe your relationship with your daughter is too tense to sustain a conversation like this, let me encourage you to try the following: Pray for the supernatural ability to "begin again"—and again and again.

When there is a lull in the tension or even a moment of calm, ask your daughter one of these questions. Begin with "I know we don't talk much, but I'd really like to know if…" If your daughter rebuffs you, tell her, "I want a better relationship with you. I'm going to keep trying the best I can to let you know that I really want to know what you are feeling."

I know that trying again in the face of a sullen or shut-down daughter is a task of heroic proportions. But what is the alternative?

expresses interest in different religious, political, or lifestyle ideas, and a parent responds with shock and condemnation, a girl may feel "sentenced" to the more quiet, desperate expression of herself through self-injury.

Although self-injury is almost always done in private and kept hidden, it clearly conveys a message for others to receive. The girl who injures herself wants someone to care about her loss as much as she does, and she wants to be able to communicate all that she is feeling without condemnation. Unfortunately, self-injuring behavior usually has a counterproductive result: It frightens parents and alienates girls even further from family and friends.

THE PATH TO RECOVERY

Girls who injure themselves need help from a therapist or a treatment program. Often, getting your daughter onto the healing path is a formidable task, but it is one of the greatest gifts you will give her. If you suspect your daughter is self-injuring, *pay attention!* Ignoring the behavior will not make it go away. If you suspect she is cutting, begin your journey together on the path to recovery by saying, "I'm very worried about you. I've seen the scars and marks on your arms/legs, and I'm afraid you may be hurting yourself. Please know you can talk to me about this. I won't freak out, and you won't be in trouble. I just want to help. I have a few ideas, but I want to know what you are thinking first."

Hopefully, this chapter has helped you understand a little more about self-injury and led you to grapple with your own response of shock, horror, anger, fear, guilt, or disgust. When you can let go of these feelings, you can approach your daughter with compassion, understanding, and strength. If your daughter doesn't want to talk about the cutting, tell her you know she deserves to talk to someone, and take her to a therapist who understands self-injury. If your daughter resists treatment, tell her that you hope she's right about this not being a problem and that you want to get a third party to confirm her downplaying of the behavior. Give your daughter input and choices in finding a therapist. Tell her that you will schedule an appointment for her to interview three different therapists and that she can choose the one that she wants to see (see "Finding Caregivers for Your Daughter" on page 206).

For Holly, working with a therapist she trusted provided a safe place for her to tell her parents about the sexual abuse at camp. When she witnessed her parents' anger at the abuser and their sorrow and compassion for her, she realized that she had misjudged them. Her parents notified the authorities at the camp about the sexual abuse, asked them to take action, and indicated that if action wasn't taken, they would have to find another way to hold the abuser accountable. Her parents' actions affirmed Holly's worth, and her self-injury stopped.

The single most important guideline you need to keep in mind when guiding your daughter toward recovery is this: Do whatever you can to let your daughter know that she is not the only person affected by her self-injuring behavior. When she knows you are concerned for her and can't ignore her behavior, her resistance to getting help will diminish. The founders of SAFE concur: "We have found that once the self-injurer begins to grasp the magnitude of the impact on everyone she knows and cares about, her resistance erodes, and her motivation to change is galvanized."[8]

Blair continues to struggle with self-injury, as her family continues to struggle with "lookism." Blair has seen the impact of her cutting on her family, but sadly they have not acknowledged the impact of their preoccupation with prestige and outward appearance on Blair. When our daughters are angry or in pain, we often cannot take away their struggles. We are, however, responsible to look at ourselves first and make whatever changes are necessary to provide an environment that allows our daughters to flourish. I pray the day will come when Blair's parents read her painful hieroglyphics and understand what she is desperately trying to tell them.

Understanding the roles of a sense of belonging and loss, the importance of self-expression, and the impact of a rigid code of values may compel you to make some changes at home. You may need to apologize to your daughter. I am always amazed by the radically redemptive results that come with a simple apology. Our children do not need us to be perfect, but they do need us to acknowledge when we are wrong or when we unwittingly fail them.

An apology was the turning point in Marina's story. Her mother apologized for all the good grades she'd overlooked, for all the ups and downs of Marina's social life that she'd missed, for all the times that her sister's needs had eclipsed her own. She asked Marina to express her hurt and disappointment and not hold back. They cried together and decided to spend every Sunday afternoon together just hanging out. They even signed up for a watercolor painting class.

For about six months Marina and her mother paid intentional attention to their relationship and worked together with a therapist. After that time Marina gave her mother the following poem. This poem reminds me of the amazing resilience of our daughters to forgive and move forward and of the rich treasure inside teenage girls that all too often goes unexpressed because no one is listening.

When I want to escape
To a place where I
Know I'll be heard,
Where I can cry and
It will be okay,
Where I can be myself
And that will be okay too…
All I know to do
Is to find you.[9]

—MARINA

Chapter 11

Depression

*Understanding…depression in a family requires more than genetic map-
ping, family diagrams, or symptom checklists. Each of us is a complex
weaving of genes and expectations, biochemistry and family myths, and
the configuration of our family's strengths, as well as its vulnerabilities. To
truly appreciate the complexity of the weave, we have to sort out the con-
tributions of individual threads to the overall design.*

—Martha Manning, "The Legacy"

I think your daughter is depressed." I looked into the faces of the mom and
dad sitting on the couch in my office. Their daughter, Mallory, had been
seeing me for counseling for the past two months. Her parents sought counseling for Mallory because her grades had dropped from straight As to mostly
Cs and Ds. Mallory spent a lot of time in her room by herself. She'd become
increasingly irritable with her younger brother and was dropping out of family life. Mallory had confided in me that she sometimes wondered what the
point was in even living. She had no interests, goals, or close relationships.

Mallory's mom started to cry. "This is probably all my fault. I should
have been more sympathetic when she started expressing unhappiness with
her life."

"It's not our fault," her dad chided. "We have given Mallory everything
she could have possibly needed or even wanted. I don't understand why she
doesn't see her potential. What are you suggesting we do?" He looked at me.

"I think it's time to get a medical evaluation and consider the possibility
of antidepressant medication."

Mallory's dad crossed his arms and sat back on the couch. Her mom
stared at the office floor. After a few moments she blurted out, "This scares

me. Will Mallory grow up to have a normal life? Will she be branded with a label wherever she goes?"

I didn't answer this mom's fear-filled questions immediately. A diagnosis of depression is not as dark and mysterious as it used to be. Most people understand that depression is a fairly common experience and a treatable condition. However, when it is *your* child who is diagnosed with depression, fear and "horribilization" are natural reactions. I have discovered that information and the desire for a daughter to be freed from the torment of depression help parents overcome fear.

Mallory's dad pulled out his Day-Timer and started to write. "I'm going to call a friend of mine who is a doctor. We don't want to rush into anything that might affect Mallory for the rest of her life. We'll get back to you."

Mallory's dad stood up and started for the door. Her mom and I looked at each other for a few seconds. I saw the fear and confusion she felt, but I saw something else in her eyes as well: a spark of longing for her daughter. We both knew that Mallory was suffering. We both had seen Mallory's sadness, apathy, and even anger and had watched her turn those emotions inward to the point that she was tormented in her private emotional world by persistent thoughts of the unhappiness and worthlessness of her life. We both knew Mallory needed help.

Mallory's parents' misunderstanding of and resistance to a diagnosis of depression threatened to keep them from helping their daughter find not only relief from her anguish but also a pathway to a life worth living. In this chapter we will distinguish normal adolescent moodiness from depression, examine the misunderstandings that can keep parents from becoming their daughters' allies in battling depression, and look at ways parents can help.

UNDERSTANDING ADOLESCENT DEPRESSION

Most teenage girls are moody, and their ever-changing emotions may seem crazy and may even make us question our own sanity at times. But adolescence is not a morass of only negative emotions and depressed and even self-destructive thoughts. For some girls, however, they get stuck in a case of the blues, and they become trapped in thoughts of despair and self-destruction.

Experts in the field of adolescent psychology believe that 20 percent of all teenagers will have a diagnosable depression at some time during their adolescence.

A diagnosis of major depression will be made if the depressed person's feelings of sadness, or consistent loss of interest or pleasure, have gone on for at least two weeks, and if four of the following six difficulties have occurred almost every day: appetite problems; sleep problems; lack of energy; feelings of worthlessness, hopelessness or guilt; difficulty concentrating; suicidal thoughts or attempts."[1]

About three out of every ten teens will experience mild to moderate depressive symptoms, which actually parallels the statistics for adult depression.[2] When an adolescent depressive episode is untreated, that teenager is much more likely to experience an even more intense depressive episode as an adult. But a greater understanding of teen depression might result in a reduction of adult depression. Helping your daughter identify and treat depression now will not only model to her how to deal with her depression if it resurfaces later, but it may prevent depression from recurring in adulthood.

How can you recognize if your daughter is depressed? How many times does your daughter have to say, "Mom, I hate my life!" before you should become alarmed? Clinical depression compels us to address biology first. For a number of reasons in both teens and adults—stress, trauma, loss, physical illness, and so on—the chemicals in the brain that pass messages between the brain and other nerve cells are not produced in sufficient quantities. Receptors on the cells either activate or suppress specific activity. Receptors are like the locks on the doors of cells. Neurotransmitters (brain chemicals) are the keys to the locks. If neurotransmitters are not adequately produced, the doors to the cells stay locked, shutting down brain activities like the production of a sense of well-being, feeling good, or being able to focus. This, of course, is a simplistic explanation of the complex wiring in the brain and what goes awry in depression. You can read further about the biology of depression in some of the books listed in the section titled "Finding Caregivers for Your Daughter" on page 206.

Although brain chemistry explains your daughter's depression, her behaviors will be the first clues you get that something is wrong. Listed on the following pages are indicators for adolescent depression. This is not a diagnostic tool but rather a way for you to identify what might be going on with your daughter in order to see more clearly what you can do to best help her.

Listed below are two sets of indicators: *Indicators That Need Watching* and *Indicators That Require Action.* If your daughter's symptoms fall in the first category, you will want to be vigilant in making sure that these symptoms don't turn into the indicators listed in the second group. Go back to the definition of clinical (major) depression on page 163. If you see at least four of these indicators every day for two weeks, you will want to consult your doctor and find a counselor to help your daughter talk through some of the things she is feeling.

If your daughter's symptoms fall in the second category, you will want to get a medical evaluation from a physician who knows about adolescent depression as well as find a counselor for your daughter who is experienced in treating teen depression.

Your physician will perform a few blood tests to make sure there are no indicators of other physical illness. He or she will then refer you to an adolescent psychiatrist who will assess your daughter's depression by asking diagnostic questions and probably administering a questionnaire that will help further define her depression. Ideally, your physician and psychiatrist should confer in order to recommend the best treatment for your daughter, including medication and therapy (see "Finding Caregivers for Your Daughter" on page 206).

Indicators That Need Watching
- a decline in academic performance
- dropping out of sports, hobbies, church activities
- apathy about trying anything new
- social isolation
- complaints about feeling fat or ugly
- irritability with family member(s)
- withdrawing from family life
- fatigue, lethargy
- difficulty concentrating, remembering responsibilities, making decisions
- persistent headaches or unexplained body pains

- complaints about feeling left out or victimized by others
- stomachaches, nausea, nervous stomach
- binging, chronic dieting, or other disordered eating patterns
- chronic anxiety
- sleep problems
- persistent sadness, crying spells
- sense of worthlessness
- diminished attention to personal hygiene

Indicators That Require Action
- self-harming behaviors (cutting, burning, exercising to the point of exhaustion)
- significant changes in eating behavior (binging, purging, starving)
- chronic sleep problems (for more than two or three weeks)
- substance abuse
- sexual promiscuity (This can include becoming sexually active when that has been against your daughter's values in the past, or having indiscriminate sex with lots of partners.)
- running away from home or school
- increased irritability to the point of fighting, yelling, or alienating others (for more than two or three weeks)
- apathy that results in school failure, dropping out of sports or hobbies (for more than two or three weeks)
- increased anxiety that results in fear of health problems, fear of peers, fear of social situations, etc. (for more than two or three weeks)
- recurring thoughts of death or suicide
- plans for or an attempt at suicide

Teenagers get depressed for the same reasons adults do. Teen depression develops in the context of *biology* and *biography*. The causes and treatments are the same, but there are some differences in the "presentation" of depression. One confusing difference is that teens can often find the energy for social activities even when they are depressed, while a depressed adult might drop out of social life entirely. Adolescents experience difficulty in articulating what they are feeling, especially at the beginning of the continuum of depression. This is not much different from adults; however, teenagers often do not have previous experiences with loss or grief and may not even realize that they are feeling sad. Adults often feel embarrassed when they are diagnosed with depression (which influences their response to their daughters' depression). Teenagers usually don't feel embarrassed, but they may feel angry, thinking that the depression has been inflicted on them.

Adolescence is the time when the "depression gene" might get turned on in the brain due to changing hormone levels. Hormone levels affect the production of brain chemicals (neurotransmitters) that control brain activity. The fluctuation of hormone levels in teen brains can have a direct effect, making teens more excitable and vulnerable to sudden mood changes. This hormonal fluctuation may slow down or speed up the production of neurotransmitters, resulting in the doors to the cells that produce good feelings as well as agitated feelings either being locked all the time or ajar all the time. Antidepressants regulate brain chemistry so that neurotransmitters lock and unlock cell doors appropriately. Whether a teenager is susceptible to depression because of genetic vulnerabilities (it runs in the family) or changing hormonal levels that play havoc with the emotions (it's part of being a teenager), biology is a significant factor in the onset of clinical depression.

The biography of a teenager may include many chapter titles that indicate the possibility for depression: transition to high school, loss of a grandparent, scary and challenging world events, breakup with a boyfriend, a family move, parents' divorce. These life experiences change brain chemistry, impacting the production of neurotransmitters. Many adults and teenagers can "bounce back" from life difficulties without becoming depressed. One factor in resilience is temperament; some girls are optimistic and easygoing by nature. Being able to do things well—in school or extracurricular activities—also seems to protect against depression. When biology, biography, and the absence of protective factors collide, however, your daughter may become depressed.

Both biology and biography impact your daughter's emotional well-being, and both contribute to the possibility of her struggling with depression. The following exercises in "Just for You" and "Just for the Two of You" will help you and your daughter get a picture of some of the factors that contribute to your daughter's depression. Use the following tools to assure your daughter (and yourself) that there are legitimate reasons for her emotional turmoil.

JUST FOR YOU

Fill out the "family tree" diagrammed below. What does it suggest about your daughter's biological vulnerability to depression? Fill in as much information as you can. If you don't have a thorough history of your family's mental health, be sure to include all that you can about your own experience. Fill in your family history for depression beginning with your primary relationships and working backward. Circle the names of those you know who have struggled with depression. Put a star (*) by the names of people with struggles such as "nervous breakdown," suicide, addictions, or other identifiable dysfunctions.

Child's Biological Father:

_____

Child's Biological Mother:

_____

Father's Parents:

Father_____

Mother_____

Mother's Parents:

Father_____

Mother_____

Siblings

_____

_____

_____

Siblings

_____

_____

_____

Nephews/Nieces

_____

_____

_____

Nephews/Nieces

_____

_____

_____

Aunts/Uncles

_____

_____

_____

Aunts/Uncles

_____

_____

_____

(continued on the following page)

You may want to consider telling your daughter some of the family stories of struggle, if you know them, and help her see the genetic "roots" of her own struggles.

If you have battled depression, now is the time to clearly understand your own struggle. Children of depressed parents show a higher lifetime risk of major depression. The risk of depression is higher if it is the mother who was depressed.[3] Ask yourself the following questions:

- Looking back, when did I first experience depression?
- What did my parents do about it? What did I do? What do I wish we would have done?
- What made me ask for help? If I didn't get help, why not?
- How did I feel when a doctor or counselor suggested that I was depressed?
- How did I feel when a doctor prescribed medication?
- What helped me get better?
- How do I know now when I am starting to get depressed?
- What do I do to take care of myself?

Just for the Two of You

The following checklist indicates possible "life stressors." Fill out the checklist together and talk about the contributing factors that might be influencing your daughter's emotional struggles. If your daughter doesn't want to talk about these things, observe as much as you can about what is going on with her to arm yourself with information for her doctor and therapist.

____ death of a family member

____ death of a friend

____ divorce of parents

____ problems in parents' marriage

____ personal serious illness or injury

____ moving

____ new sibling or other family members (through birth, adoption, or blending families)

____ changing friend group

____ breaking up with boyfriend

___ getting a D or F in a class at school	___ fighting with best friend
___ changing schools	___ trouble with teacher
___ a parent's loss of job	___ harassment by peers
___ change in standard of living	___ major physical change
___ experimenting with alcohol	___ parent getting remarried
___ sister or brother leaving home	___ getting a job
___ ending of an athletic season	___ trouble on the job
___ finishing major project, hobby	___ experimenting with drugs
___ leaving church or youth group	___ sexual relationship
	___ sister or brother in trouble
	___ friend in trouble
	___ world problems

TEEN DEPRESSION AND SUBSTANCE ABUSE

It can be difficult to distinguish a depressed teen from an adolescent who is using drugs or abusing alcohol. Poor grades, problems with memory and concentration, change in appetite, and alienation from family and friends are some of the symptoms that are similar. Some theorists believe that depressed teenagers abuse drugs or alcohol to self-medicate their depression. Others argue that substance abuse causes depression. All agree that substance abuse intensifies depression and puts a teenager at serious risk for harm.

The checklists below will aid you in determining whether your teen is abusing drugs or alcohol. If you suspect your daughter is a substance abuser, seek information, counsel, and help immediately.

Physical Indicators
___ the smell of alcohol, nicotine, or marijuana
___ nicotine-stained fingers (Although many teens smoke who are not depressed, nicotine is a mood-altering drug and should be taken into consideration when assessing your daughter's depression.)
___ dilated pupils
___ chronic cough

___ altered behavior

___ appetite change

Psychological Indicators

___ loss of enjoyment in previously enjoyed activities

___ withdrawal

___ irritability

___ mood swings

___ social changes—dropping old friends, new friends

___ increased anxiety

___ secretive behavior

Spiritual Indicators

___ withdrawal from participation in church

___ anger toward God

___ sense of guilt

___ focus on drug culture—friends, music, movies

___ detachment from or contempt for family values

One of my friends began to watch her daughter closely for evidence of depression when her daughter unexpectedly quit the soccer team. Soccer had always brought her daughter a lot of joy and satisfaction, so when she quit, my friend wondered what was going on. Her usually open daughter became secretive, and my friend became more alarmed when she discovered a crumpled pack of cigarettes under her daughter's bed.

As she tried to talk to her daughter, she was met with terse answers and a closed demeanor. This "detective mom" kept her eyes open and did not become reactive to her daughter. She prayed a lot as she observed her bright-eyed girl becoming duller in affect and confusing in her choice of friends and activities.

One Sunday morning when her daughter refused to go to church, my friend stayed home to try to get some answers. She brought her daughter breakfast in bed and said, "I'm sure something hard is going on in your life. Please talk to me."

My friend's prayers, observations, and pleas paid off. Her daughter began to talk about a broken friendship with a teammate and some cruel criticism from her soccer coach. Her temperament had contributed to her keeping this all inside, resulting in a confusing mix of pain and anger. She gravitated to a different peer group as a reaction to the broken friendship. When she started smoking, she discovered a little relief. The rebellion felt powerful, but the nicotine also released chemicals in her brain that produced moments of calm and well-being. She was self-medicating her growing depression with a temporary, ultimately harmful remedy.

My friend started to talk about depression from her own experience. As soon as her daughter heard about the symptoms, it was as if a light went on. *"That's* what I have!" She wanted to see a doctor immediately. She was a little more reluctant to get counseling, but agreed to follow the doctor's recommendations.

In the weeks that followed, my friend not only took her daughter to therapy and reminded her to take her medication, but she also regularly scheduled a massage, manicure, movie, hike, or shopping expedition. She told her daughter, "This is like taking your medication. You have to do it, but we might as well enjoy the treatment!" She modeled for her daughter how to treat her depression proactively.

Not all teens are as "easy" as my friend's daughter, but my experience is that most respond to a nonjudgmental description of depression. Depression does not have all the "baggage" for teens that it has for some adults, and girls are often relieved to know that what they are experiencing has a name and that there is treatment for it. Teens are quick to latch on to something that is not their fault. When an informed description of depression is presented and relief is promised, most girls will take the first step and do what they need to do to get treatment.

When medication is offered in the context of a plan for treating the whole person—counseling, massage therapy, help with schoolwork or other difficulties—most teens will respond favorably. A mom can facilitate the process by being informed and presenting treatment as something wonderful that her daughter deserves. Even if your daughter complains, resolve to remind her to take her medication, take her to counseling, and schedule a massage with positive intention. Learn to disregard the complaints and believe in the process, even when your daughter does not.

Misunderstanding Teen Depression

When your daughter complains of an upset stomach, a sore throat, or a fever, you wouldn't think of blaming yourself for her illness. You would not catastrophize the situation and believe that the rest of her life will be ruined because she is sick. You wouldn't be afraid or ashamed of what others might think. And you wouldn't be reluctant to get medication that might relieve your daughter's symptoms and help her get well.

But depression is different, isn't it? I agree that emotional distress is more confusing and frightening than some physical ailments. Our daughters' serious emotional lows and their potential to lead to self-destructive behaviors should alarm us, but not to the point of adopting outdated and wrong thinking about depression. Depression is a sickness that impacts the sense of self, mood, and beliefs about the future. Depression is an illness that affects every part of a person's life. Poet Jane Kenyon describes her reality after the onset of a major depressive episode: "And from that day on / everything under the sun and moon / made me sad."[4]

Mallory's parents responded to the possibility of their daughter's depression with common sentiments from parents who misunderstand depression: "It's all my fault," "This is horrible," and "She doesn't need medication." The rest of this chapter is dedicated to encouraging parents to accept their daughter's depression and respond in ways that will help her get better.

"It's All My Fault"

We mothers are especially quick to blame ourselves for anything that goes wrong with our children. We remember when we yelled, were too busy, or dismissed our daughters' concerns. Harriet Lerner, acclaimed expert on the psychology of women, writes that "one thing [that mothers] learn on the job is guilt." But she wisely concludes, "The guilt ingrained in mothers is usually not the productive variety."[5]

Lerner's words are especially apropos to a discussion of depression. Mothers who don't blame themselves are better able to help their daughters. In fact, your daughter will probably sense your compassion and confidence that this illness can be treated and feel reassured that the depression is no one's fault—hers or yours.

JUST FOR YOU

Sometimes guilt is good. It indicates that there is something we need to seek forgiveness for. Get a stack of index cards. On each card write one thing you feel guilty about with regard to your daughter's life. List as many distinct guilty feelings as you can. Now let's dissect your guilt. Begin by separating your "guilt cards" into two piles: "Things I can do something about" and "Things I can't do anything about."

Set aside the stack of cards that you can do something about. Do you need to apologize? give your daughter more attention? be more compassionate? Prayerfully commit to doing whatever you can. The remaining stack of cards is evidence of your false guilt. Chances are these nagging feelings of guilt have to do with things you cannot control or things that don't have anything to do with you. Release yourself from the "guilt trips" on these cards so that you will be available for what you *can* do with your daughter.

"THIS IS HORRIBLE"

The stigma of depression and the fear that depression is something horrible that cannot be successfully treated are outmoded ways of thinking that are rooted in a misunderstanding of depression. Writing more than a decade ago, Dr. Gregory Jantz reported, "In the past fifteen years, the number of people in the U.S. suffering from depression has more than doubled.... Across the globe, by the year 2020, depression is projected to be second only to heart disease as the leading cause of debilitating illness."[6] Medical and mental health caregivers understand depression as a real illness that is successfully treatable. Employers and educational institutions are prohibited, by law, from discriminating against those who suffer from depression.

Adolescents who have been diagnosed with depression and treated lead not only productive lives but also lives with greater compassion for others because of their own suffering. In fact, the tragic symptoms that we often associate with depression—self-destruction, isolation, and suicide—are the results of *unidentified* and *untreated* depression. The most important gifts we can give to our children when they suffer are the courage to identify and acknowledge the truth and the strength to pursue healing and health.

Please know that when you deny or ignore your daughter's depression, you are participating in the possibility that this often-recurring struggle will hit her again later in life with even greater force. Untreated clinical depression changes brain chemistry and sets forces in motion that virtually guarantee that the next bout with depression will be more severe.[7]

I'm hardly carefree—I still scan myself for depression as if checking for broken bones. But I consider my ability to participate at last in the everyday a gift. I don't know where depression comes from or where it goes. I do know that it was the crucible, the rite of passage, that allowed me to create my life.

—Lesley Dormen, "Planet No" in *Unholy Ghost: Writers on Depression*

When you ally yourself with your daughter and seek a medical evaluation, insist on counseling, and encourage your daughter to take care of herself while she is in this vulnerable time by getting massages, paying attention to her physical health, and spending time with friends, you model for her how important it is to ask for help when she is in need. You put a real-life perspective on Jesus's words, "Blessed are the poor in spirit, for theirs is the kingdom of heaven. Blessed are those who mourn, for they will be comforted" (Matthew 5:3-4, NIV).

"My Daughter Doesn't Need Medication"
Often this misunderstanding is merged with other unhelpful sentiments such as "She just needs to snap out of this" or "She must not be walking closely with God." Because clinical depression is often rooted in biological imbalances, it is often essential that these imbalances be restored through medication. Of course, you don't want your daughter to be "doped up," and you don't want unnecessary medication. But Dr. Miriam Kaufman, staff physician with the Division of Adolescent Medicine at The Hospital for Sick Children, explains, "It is becoming clear that depression...is caused by chemical disturbances or imbalances in the brain, and it makes sense that medications are going to be the best treatment for this condition."[8]

Dr. Kaufman pleads for parents to get a medical assessment for their child if he or she has experienced, for at least two weeks, four of the following six difficulties: appetite problems; sleep problems; lack of energy; feelings of worthlessness, hopelessness or guilt; difficulty concentrating; suicidal thoughts or attempts.[9] I ask my clients to track their moods on a calendar and rate their negative feelings (anger, sadness, hopelessness, etc.) on a scale of 1 to 10, indicating if something specific is happening to influence the number. This tool can be used as part of the medical evaluation to get a picture of how the teen is feeling, not just on the day of the appointment but overall.

Your doctor or psychiatrist will help you understand how medication works, possible side effects, and when and how to stop medication. Adolescents usually take antidepressants for less than a year and often realize significant improvements in their quality of life. Teens still have relatively healthy brains that can recover quickly. They are also more willing to believe that things can improve sooner because they have experienced less failure and disappointment than adults have.[10]

Medication is only one part of the treatment plan along with counseling and family support. Treatment may also include acupuncture, exercise, a nutritional plan and dietary supplements, massage therapy, and volunteer work. Some of these "alternative" treatments, whether or not they work directly on the depression, may help speed recovery by giving teens a sense that they are taking control over their depression.

Mallory's parents began a crash course in learning about depression and did seek medical treatment for Mallory. They read books, attended a class on adolescent depression at the hospital, and interviewed three psychiatrists who were recommended by their doctor before picking one for Mallory. After two months on medication and in counseling, Mallory started to participate in life again. She started to focus on her grades and took pride in her accomplishments. She joined the track team at school and enjoyed the sport, the camaraderie, and the physical exercise. She still experiences bouts of melancholy (normal for human beings) and gets mad at her younger brother, but she is hopeful that life holds possibilities, not just problems.

Regardless of the treatment plan, you may find that your daughter resists the treatment. In the following "Just for the Two of You" section you will find a list of exercises that may help both you and your daughter reframe your attitudes about treatment.

JUST FOR THE TWO OF YOU

1. Write down some of the negative responses you or your daughter has to the prescribed treatment. For example, "Antidepressants are for weak people," "You should be able to just snap out of this," or "You're just not spiritual enough."

2. Write out the truth that answers each negative response, using the information in this chapter and other resources on depression (see the resources section on page 209).

3. Find someone (either in person or in writing) who has struggled with depression and overcome it with treatment, and take note of what helped them. Can you learn and apply anything from their story?

4. Build in evaluation times as part of your daughter's treatment plan. Tell her that if she does not feel better in eight weeks, you will seek another professional opinion. If you used a calendar to track her moods, continue this practice after she begins treatment. This can help you evaluate whether there is a change, even a small one, in the number of days she is significantly affected by a depressed mood.

5. Remind your daughter (and yourself) that following a treatment plan can be a matter of life or death. You may have to remind her to take her medication each day and be relentless in encouraging her to follow the treatment plan. The treatment, recommended by doctors and therapists, can help stabilize the situation and possibly prevent suicide.

THE BEST REMEDY

When your daughter is lost in a struggle that threatens her well-being and scrambles her perspective, you have the opportunity to give her a pearl of great price: a sense of belonging. Depression makes its sufferers feel isolated, ashamed, and worthless. The antidote for these maladies is *belonging*. As you arm yourself with information about depression, find a doctor and therapist who understand teen depression and relate well to your daughter, and encourage (nag) your daughter to take her medication, you may feel overwhelmed, unqualified, discouraged, and sometimes afraid. However, giving your daughter a sense of belonging is something you can do no matter how limited your understanding of depression is or how tired and frustrated you become in the battle. And as you tell your daughter that she belongs, remind yourself that you belong to the One who said, "Fear not, for I have redeemed you; I have summoned you by name; you are mine" (Isaiah 43:1, NIV).

Imagine what would happen if you whispered to your lonely, sullen, awkward daughter, "You belong to me. I love you. Nothing can change my love for you."

How do you think your daughter—your despairing, angry, ashamed daughter—would feel if you reminded her, "Some of the greatest artists, writers, and leaders in the world have suffered from depression. You belong to an honorable company"?

What if you told your daughter, even though she's irritable and hard to be around, the following: "More than half of the psalms are cries of despair and anguish. What you are feeling doesn't mean you're unspiritual. You belong in the company of others who think about life deeply and honestly"?

Might your daughter relax, even though she's acting out or withdrawing, if you told her, "You belong in our family. We want you. Nothing will ever change our love for you"?

Depression is a formidable foe that will confuse you, stretch you to try things you haven't tried before, frighten you, and test your faith in yourself, your daughter, the medical experts, your daughter's caregivers, and even your faith in God's power and care for you and your daughter. Sometimes you won't know what to do, and you'll be afraid that nothing is working. Belonging is the remedy that you can always return to, always rely on, and always offer your hurting daughter. She belongs to you, to a company of fellow sufferers, to your family, to God.

Depression teaches us that we are not immune from the pain of life. Our daughters learn from our responses to the tests of life as much as they learn from the actual tests. My goal is no longer to handle it all perfectly. How else will my daughter ever learn that she doesn't have to be perfect herself? If my daughter struggles with depression and even gets lost in it or struggles with any of the other ways life tests our faith, hope, and love, I wish to be for her, among other things, a sweet voice that penetrates the darkness and patiently, persistently calls her gently toward home—where she belongs.

Chapter 12

Suicide

Suicide in the young, which has at least tripled over the past forty-five years, is without argument, one of our most serious public health problems. Suicide is the third leading cause of death in young people in the United States and the second for college students.

—Kay Redfield Jamison, *Night Falls Fast*

Nobody likes me, not even my own father." Abby spoke with a flat expression that did not match the anguish of her words. "I want to kill myself. If I could figure out a way to do it—for sure—I would kill myself."

Abby's words pierced my heart and made it beat a little faster. I resisted the urge to say, "Oh, I'm sure your father likes you," or "Don't talk about killing yourself!" I wanted to wrap my arms around this beautiful, sad fourteen-year-old and tell her I would make sure that the pain of her parents' divorce, the cruelty of other teenagers, or the awkwardness of growing up never hurt her again. But instead I asked her, "Abby, do you have a plan for killing yourself?"

"No, not really," she answered. "I've thought about taking a bunch of Advil or something."

Once again I resisted my first impulse to run out into my waiting room and tell her mother to go home and hide all the Advil and, while she was at it, to throw away all the medicine in the house too. I felt an irrational urge to call the manufacturers of Advil and tell them to just stop making their product. Don't they know that teenage girls are using it to hurt themselves? I wanted to say to Abby, "Just stay with me. I don't have any Advil. You'll be safe here."

But instead I asked, "On a scale of one to ten, how much do you feel like killing yourself today?"

"I don't know. Maybe a two—today." Abby paused. "On other days I'm an eight or nine."

"Have you told your mother you are thinking about suicide?" I asked her.

"No, I can't tell her. She's got enough to worry about, with my dad leaving and all the money problems. She doesn't need to worry any more about me," Abby answered with the greatest emotion in her voice so far that hour.

"We need to tell her. She would want to know how bad you are feeling. I'll be there with you when you tell her," I promised. "I'll help you and her get through this."

THE WORD THAT STRIKES TERROR

Suicide. I don't think there is a more frightening word for parents, especially parents of teenagers who are struggling with depression. It is virtually inconceivable for those of us who have given birth to a son or a daughter to think that they might want to die. This chapter is written to mothers of girls who have whispered, "I can't do this anymore," or shouted, "I wish I was dead!" or written in their journals, "Life is not worth living."

---

*This way, love has the run of the house, becomes at home and mature
in us, so that we're free of worry.... There is no room in love for fear.
Well-formed love banishes fear. Since fear is crippling, a fearful life—
fear of death, fear of judgment—is not yet fully formed in love.*

—1 JOHN 4:17-18

First, we will look at the continuum of suicidal thought and behavior in order to help you evaluate your daughter's emotional state and needs. Then we will examine four common fearful responses to suicidal behavior and how you can transform these responses into "love in action" that casts out all fear.

THE CONTINUUM OF SUICIDAL THOUGHTS AND BEHAVIORS

"Suicide is the anchor point on a continuum of suicidal thoughts and behaviors," writes Kay Redfield Jamison in her informative and compelling book about suicide, *Night Falls Fast.*[1] The continuum ranges from expressions of a wish to die to risk-taking or self-destructive behaviors to suicidal thoughts and plans to suicide attempts and suicide.

Abby's behaviors indicate that she is somewhere between the beginning of the continuum and the middle. The continuum is hard to measure in teenagers because we are often unsure of their intent. Are they trying to scare us or get our attention? Do they really mean to kill themselves, or are they just pretending to think about suicide in order to get some desired response?

We will not explore how to measure suicide intent in this chapter. Experts in adolescent psychology have devised means that enable mental health professionals to evaluate suicide intent and assess those at risk. The following "Just for You" section provides a list of some of the risk factors for suicide that you should be aware of. If your daughter is expressing suicidal thoughts or behaviors, you need to make an appointment with a psychiatrist who can professionally assess your daughter's suicide intent.

JUST FOR YOU

Foundational risk factors for suicide are more general indicators that increase a teen's vulnerability to specific stressors or events that pose immediate risks for suicide. These include:

- psychiatric disorders, including depression or substance abuse
- a previous suicide attempt
- the suicide of a family member
- the suicide of a friend

Immediate risk factors for suicide include the following:

- the death of a parent or close friend
- trouble with the police
- breaking up with a boyfriend or ending a close friendship
- family breakup
- bullying or harassment
- sexual or physical assault[2]

When risk factors alert you that your daughter is in trouble, understanding where she is on the continuum of suicidal thought or behavior will further guide you to getting the right kind of help for her.

Although you can't definitively measure your daughter's intent to commit suicide, you can be continually assessing the factors that can give clues about her emotional health and will arm you with information to give her physician or psychiatrist.

"I Wish I Could Just Die"

Expressions of a wish to die are relatively common among adolescents. Girls often express these wishes in the midst of a dramatic time of life. Mothers

Just for You

If your daughter is expressing thoughts about suicide, ask her if she is thinking about killing herself. Watch for evasive answers or nonanswers such as "Why would you ask me that?" or "Don't you trust me?" If she admits she is thinking about suicide, tell her that she doesn't have to feel guilty about her pain and that it isn't her fault. Tell her that there is help and you will seek it together immediately. Make an appointment with a therapist who works with depressed adolescents. If your daughter is evasive, tell her you understand that it's hard to talk about painful or shocking feelings and that you are making an appointment for both of you to talk to someone who can help you sort things out.

This is the time to shower your daughter with love and affection. Let her know how much you love her. Tell her specific things you love about her. Tell her how much she has enriched your life and how devastated you would be without her.

Lock up all the medication in your home. This may seem like a dramatic response, but it is a necessary one at the beginning of the continuum. A high percentage of adolescent girls' suicide attempts involve the ingestion of medication. If your daughter is expressing thoughts of suicide, do not take the risk that she might not be serious. If she asks about your locking up the medication, tell her, "I am taking your words seriously and don't want to have anything around the house that you might be able to use to harm yourself." If she becomes angry or defensive, calmly assure her that you are not judging her but are loving her by taking her words seriously.

need to distinguish between drama and emotional distress. The statement "I wish I could just die" that a girl expresses after an embarrassing situation with her peers is different from the pain-filled words a girl writes in her journal: "The world would be better off without me."

The beginning of the continuum of suicidal thoughts and behaviors is the best time to bring this subject out into the light. If your daughter is talking or writing about dying, chances are that she is confused or worried about suicide. She may be testing the waters—bringing up the subject, in part, to see how you react. If you ignore her comments, the thoughts may take root in the soil of solitary brooding. If you cut her off or shut her down, the ideas can become a private cause that she begins to champion. If you can respond with comments that invite discussion and reveal compassion, you can help diffuse the power and allure of suicidal thoughts.

Risk-Taking or Self-Destructive Behaviors

Risk-taking behaviors for adolescent girls include abusing alcohol or drugs, being involved in sexually promiscuous activities (meeting boys through Internet connections, being sexually active, especially with relatively unknown boys, etc.), cutting or burning the skin, starving themselves. Although these behaviors are not suicide attempts, when they are presented along with other indicators of depression (see chapter 11), they are defined by experts in the field as "subintentional" suicidal behavior.[3] At this stage of the continuum, parents need to respond to these risk-taking behaviors with a kind and strong hand.

In the eyes of its mother every beetle is a gazelle.

—Moroccan Proverb

Perhaps seeing these behaviors not only as objectionable and scary but as life-devaluing behaviors will help you respond to your daughter with a fierce compassion that conveys that you know these are matters of life and death. Tell your daughter her life-risking behaviors indicate that she doesn't really believe her life is valuable. Tell her that she deserves to talk to someone who can help her value her life and go after the life she really wants. Seek professional help immediately.

Once again, now is the time to lavish your daughter with love, attention, and affirmation. This may be hard because her behaviors are not particularly inviting or lovely. Your role is to remember what is *most true* about her: She is an amazing creation of God, designed to live with purpose and dignity and to love and be loved.

SUICIDAL THOUGHTS AND PLANS

The 1997 Youth Risk Behavior Surveillance Survey canvassed 16,000 ninth through twelfth graders. The researchers discovered that one in every five of the teenagers surveyed had "seriously considered" attempting suicide in the previous twelve months; 16 percent had actually drawn up a plan. Girls were much more likely to have considered or planned a suicide attempt.[4] This last statistic may surprise you because further statistics from the same survey suggest that boys are more "successful" at committing suicide than girls. The reality that girls are more intentional and thoughtful about ending their lives increases the opportunity for intervention.

There is a crack in everything. That's how the light gets in.

—LEONARD COHEN, "Anthem"

Kay Redfield Jamison writes that "most instances of suicidal thought, although often frightening and of concern, lead to neither a suicide attempt nor suicide, but some do."[5] Mothers of daughters who express suicidal thoughts or plans need to take firm and loving action. Find your daughter a therapist. Write down the therapist's phone number, your phone number, and the phone number of a trusted friend, and give it to your daughter to keep with her. Get her a prepaid phone card or cell phone so that she will have the means to call someone if she feels suicidal. Do not avoid talking with your daughter about her suicidal thoughts or plans. Tell her you want to know what she is thinking. Assure her that she won't get in trouble. Ask her to give you advice on how you can best help her when she's feeling this way.

After Abby and I shared with her mother the suicidal thoughts and plans Abby was contemplating, Abby's mom began a daily, intentional practice of addressing Abby's feelings. She did not shy away from Abby's feelings or make her feel guilty or ashamed for thinking about suicide. In conjunction with weekly therapy, this mom's love in action began to get the message across to Abby that she mattered, that her mom would listen to Abby's feelings, and that they could get through this together. Following are some of the things Abby and her mother did during this crisis of emotion:

- Abby's mom asked her to write about her feelings every day, or if she didn't feel like writing, to draw a picture that reflected her emotional state. They set aside time to talk about the journal entries and pictures. When they noticed a downward trend over several days, Abby brought the pictures and writings to her therapist. Abby and her mother learned that suicidal feelings almost always lift with time and tender loving care.

- Abby's mom asked her to write a letter each week to a person who hypothetically might be thinking about killing herself. Her mom used the letter to gather clues to Abby's internal world. She also took note of the reasons for living that Abby wrote to this "friend" and reminded Abby of her own words and feelings about living during hard days.

- When Abby expressed suicidal thoughts, her mom asked her to promise that she wouldn't act on those thoughts that day. She didn't ask her to promise never to kill herself (although she wanted to) because that promise is not meaningful to an adolescent. She also asked Abby to promise that she would talk with her in person before attempting any suicidal behavior. The "in person" part is important.

- Abby and her mom learned that nature is especially calming and encouraging to those who struggle with depression. Abby's mom remembered that Abby had always wanted a dog. She had resisted the idea because of the mess and work of having a pet. Her love for her daughter, however, quickly overcame any worries about pet stains and dog hair. Together Abby and her mom researched dogs and settled on a yellow Labrador retriever. Abby's care and love for her dog became an important avenue for her own healing. When Abby's mom watches her play or cuddle with her dog, she gives thanks for that hairy, smelly creature that brought light into her daughter's dark world.

SUICIDE ATTEMPTS AND SUICIDE

At the end of the continuum, you may experience the terrifying, heartbreaking reality of an attempted suicide. Your daughter may ingest pills or attempt to slice her wrists. If this happens, you may not only fear for your daughter and her pain, but you may feel your own pain—and possibly shame. As you get help for your daughter, don't neglect yourself. Find a professional and/or support group to help you work through your own emotions and fears.

JUST FOR THE TWO OF YOU

When your daughter is in a more talkative mood, ask her about the things in her life she would change if she could. Write down each item in one column.

In a second column write what you and your daughter can do to bring about the desired change.

If something seems unchangeable, tell your daughter you will pray about it and look at other resources to see if you can come up with an idea for change.

Follow through.

When your daughter is feeling increased despair, remind her of the changes that have already taken place, and ask her if there is something new she wants to add to her list.

TRANSFORMING FEARFUL RESPONSES

Suicidal behavior is a terrifying answer to emotional turmoil that naturally provokes a fear-filled response from parents. Even with a good therapist and good tools for keeping the lines of communication open, the idea that your child is contemplating suicide will still stop you in your tracks. You will be afraid. You will say the wrong thing. But if you add only your own fears to your daughter's angst, the result will be a mix of anxiety and anger that will not guide your daughter to safety or emotional maturity.

Remember that your daughter does not need you to respond perfectly, but she does need you to respond. In the rest of this chapter we will look at four responses that will get in the way of your becoming your daughter's ally during this distressing time. We will also look at how these responses can be transformed into life-giving action.

Perhaps everything terrible is in its deepest being something helpless that wants help from us.

—RAINER MARIA RILKE, *Letters to a Young Poet*

"SHE JUST WANTS ATTENTION"

I don't know where we got the idea that giving our children attention can be a bad thing. Certainly when our daughters' hearts are filled with angst and their minds are filled with self-destructive ideas, they need all the attention we can give them. The quiz in the "Just for You" section that follows is designed to help you evaluate how much attention you are paying to your daughter. The purpose of these questions is not to make you feel guilty, but rather to motivate you to transform your doubt- and fear-filled heart into a heart filled with curiosity and attention.

JUST FOR YOU

- What is your daughter's favorite color?
- What music does your daughter enjoy right now? What is her favorite song? Why?
- What group does your daughter belong to at school? Preppie? Techno geek? Jock?
- What is your daughter's dream car?
- What television show does your daughter watch every week?
- What television show does she hate?
- What radio station does your daughter listen to?
- What is your daughter's favorite treat?
- What accomplishment is your daughter most proud of?
- Which of your outfits does your daughter like best?

- Who are your daughter's best friends?
- What is your daughter's dream job? What job does she *not* want?
- What store is your daughter's favorite for clothes shopping?
- What words from peers have hurt your daughter?
- What boy does your daughter like?
- What does your daughter do during her off-hours at school?
- What sites on the Internet are your daughter's favorites?
- What is your daughter's screen name on the computer?
- What time does your daughter think is a fair curfew?
- What does your daughter's brother or sister do that annoys her?

If you could not answer these questions, you're not paying enough attention to your daughter. Most of the answers to these questions can be easily "caught" in daily interactions. Make note of them and use the questions or your observations to communicate to your daughter, "I see you. I listen to you. I want to know you. I pay attention to you."

"SHE'S TRYING TO MANIPULATE ME"

A girl who has suicidal thoughts or plans feels angry and powerless, so of course she is going to try to manipulate you. Her suicidal expressions are a way to express her anger at a world that hurts or rejects or confuses her. Her suicidal expressions are a way to take control over *something*. Perhaps a better question than "Is she trying to manipulate me?" is "What is she trying to manipulate me to do?"

More than any other human relationship, overwhelmingly more, motherhood means being instantly interruptible, responsive, responsible.

—TILLIE OLSEN, quoted in *O* (Oprah's magazine)

The following "Just for You" section lists what your daughter might be wanting from you and what you might give to her in response. If you suspect your daughter's suicidal thoughts and behaviors are an attempt to get something from you, what can you give? Add your own ideas to this list. Transform your suspicion into life-giving action.

Just for You

What My Daughter Wants	What I Can Give
A listening ear	Can we schedule "dates" to talk?
Attention	How can I make her feel special?
For someone to care about her pain as much as she does.	Empathy, my own tears on her behalf
For someone to set things right	Can I call a teacher or parent and ask for changes for my daughter?
Greater independence	Are there some rules we can relax?
More nurturing	Back rub, special meal
Special privileges	Is there something we can give or do for her to show her that she's special to us?

If you do discover that your daughter is thinking about or planning suicide, take it seriously. Let her know that you will take every expression of suicidal intent seriously, then follow through. If she says she's thinking about killing herself and doesn't have a plan, or that on a scale of 1 to 10, she doesn't think she's very likely to kill herself (1 to 3), follow the suggestions I mentioned earlier and get her to a therapist. Do not wait for her to mention it one more time. Let her know that her expression of suicidal thoughts is not bad, but that it is a serious reflection of internal pain she is experiencing. Express to her your desire that she get the treatment she deserves to help her feel better.

If she does have a suicide plan and exhibits any of the warning signs listed on the following page, or if she cannot reassure you that she will not kill herself, take her to a hospital emergency room immediately. The emergency

room personnel will have a psychiatrist assess your daughter and either recommend hospitalization (24–72 hours) for her protection or suggest a course
of action for you when you leave the hospital.

Warning Signs of a Potential Suicide Attempt
- Feelings of pervasive hopelessness—feelings that things won't ever
  change, that she's a failure, that life is meaningless.
- Talking about suicide.
- A sudden improvement in mood. This may be a clue that your daughter
  has come up with a plan. She may write notes to friends and family
  members expressing thanks for their love or help.
- Giving away possessions.
- Worsening depression.
- Increased substance use or abuse.
- A suicidal gesture such as taking a few pills from the medicine cabinet.
  This may be a practice run.

"She May Be Mentally Ill"

Clinical depression is a mental illness that can be treated. If your daughter is
talking about or threatening suicide and if your exasperated, anxious response
is to categorize her as mentally ill as a way to make sense of her emotional distress, then take this response to the next helpful level and seek professional
treatment for her emotional pain. Kay Redfield Jamison exhorts,

> Most who commit suicide explicitly, and often repeatedly, communi-
> cate their intentions to kill themselves to others.... For those who do
> make clear their desire to die, it is fortunate, it allows at least the possi-
> bility of treatment and prevention.[6]

I am not suggesting that the treatment of depression and suicidal thoughts
and behaviors is easy or straightforward. It may include trying several different
therapists and antidepressant medications until the best combination for your
daughter is found. The following list offers some guidelines for becoming your
daughter's ally during this time. You are not responsible to find her a "cure,"

but you are responsible to be her steadfast ally until help is found. Practicing these dos and don'ts can help you transform your fears about mental illness into a treatment plan that can relieve your daughter's pain and torment.

- *Do* take your daughter seriously.
- *Don't* leave your daughter alone when she is expressing suicidal thoughts or behaviors.
- *Do* stay calm.
- *Do* lock up all medications and potentially lethal tools (guns, knives, etc.).
- *Do* listen with eye contact and body language that suggest you are staying put and want to offer loving support.
- *Don't* promise to keep your daughter's emotional distress a secret. You may need to involve other family members or medical professionals.
- *Do* keep a list of emergency telephone numbers, her therapist's telephone number, and her doctor's number next to the telephone and in your purse.
- *Do* ask if your daughter has a plan for suicide.
- *Do* ask your daughter to "rate" her intent to commit suicide at that moment.
- *Don't* debate your daughter's feelings. Express empathy, not judgment.
- *Do* reassure your daughter that you will always love her and be there for her and that there is help available.
- *Do* remind her to take any prescribed medication.

"Maybe She Is Under Satanic Attack"

There is no doubt that the Enemy is filled with glee when any of God's children contemplate death. The apostle Paul in his letter to the church at Corinth testified of his own experience with the Messenger of Death who sought to discourage and defeat him and also wrote of his response to this attack: "Satan's angel did his best to get me down; what he in fact did was push me to my knees" (2 Corinthians 12:7).

Granted, our depressed daughters will probably not have the maturity to deepen and intensify their prayer life as a result of their suicidal thoughts. However, our daughters' depression can become an avenue by which we, as their mothers, seek God passionately and daily.

*The same parents who have ensured that their children are educated
about AIDS, sexually transmitted diseases, and drug abuse often do
not discuss the symptoms of depression, an illness that is common,
potentially lethal, and highly treatable.*

—KAY REDFIELD JAMISON, *Night Falls Fast*

I am afraid that well-meaning Christian parents who believe in the spiritual implications of suicidal thoughts and behaviors often use their spiritual beliefs as an escape from relationship. "Maybe my daughter is under satanic influence" becomes a justification to hand off a child to someone who is deemed more spiritual or who specializes in spiritual warfare. When your daughter is depressed and thinking about suicide, she definitely needs prayer,

JUST FOR YOU

You will need spiritual sustenance during this trying time for you and your daughter. Read the Psalms daily. Ask God for peace and wisdom and strength. Don't assume that "fixing" your daughter is the key to your faith in God. It is actually in the midst of emotional turmoil that you may find God's peace and comfort. God will meet you in your desperate pleadings for your daughter. He will comfort you when you're afraid. He will reveal Himself to you during the dark days of her depression.

Here are a few questions to guide you in your time of prayer and meditation in the Psalms:

- What emotions does the psalmist express?
- What are you feeling right now? Be still and examine your emotions. Express them to God.
- What might your daughter be feeling right now? Talk to God about your daughter and what she is feeling. What do you want for your daughter?
- What does the psalmist express about God?
- What do you believe about God? What do you want to believe?
- What do you trust about God? What do you want from Him?

but she also needs *you*. She doesn't need a sermon or an exhortation to trust God; she needs to know that *your* faith in God will push you to your knees in prayer for both of you. If she can't believe in God's love and power right now, tell her that you will believe for her until she can believe for herself. Transform your fears about satanic influence into prayer and faith in God that He cares for you and your daughter.

LEANING TOWARD LIFE

Marilyn found her semiconscious daughter Tamara in her bedroom, lying on top of the new blue and white comforter they had just bought at Tamara's favorite bed-and-bath store. On the floor beside the bed was an empty prescription bottle of Valium. Marilyn didn't recognize the name on the bottle and had no idea where Tamara had gotten this medication. She didn't waste time worrying about the source of this disaster. She called 911.

I had been seeing Tamara for counseling for less than two months. Her mother had done everything right. She'd watched Tamara go from being an outgoing, happy girl to a moody and increasingly melancholy adolescent. When Tamara dropped out of all activities and began spending all her time in her room with the lights turned out, her mother asked the youth pastor for help. He wisely referred her to several counselors, including me.

In the few visits I had with Tamara, I discovered that she hated high school. She didn't have any friends. Her emotional climate had gotten worse when her older sister, whom she was extremely close to, went out of state to college. I also learned that Tamara's dad had been diagnosed with bipolar disorder, a type of depression marked by extreme emotional highs and lows.

After our first counseling session, Marilyn took Tamara to a psychiatrist specialized in treating adolescents who prescribed an antidepressant. Tamara was reluctant to take the medication, so her mom had to coax her to take it on a daily basis. Marilyn watched her daughter like a hawk and took all the precautions I recommended. It was hard, agonizing mothering. Tamara seemed a little better but still would not participate in anything besides the bare minimum of going to school. Marilyn continued to ask for help from the youth staff of their church. They prayed for Tamara and invited her to all the activities, but Tamara refused to participate.

Although Marilyn asked Tamara often if she had a plan to harm herself, she didn't know that Tamara had learned that she could buy prescription pills at school. Kids who sell drugs often look for prescription medication in friends' or acquaintances' homes and steal them to sell at school. Although Tamara probably never articulated even to herself that she was planning to buy the pills and kill herself, she kept it as a growing option in the back of her mind.

On the day Tamara took the pills, I later met with her and she told me that she felt agitated and angry about seeing a counselor, taking medication, talking about her life. She was tired of being different. She had just "happened" on the place at school where "drug deals" took place, bought the Valium, left school, went home when she knew no one would be there, and took the pills. She said that she had thought about writing a note to apologize or explain, but she was just too tired of it all. She remembered lying down, and the next thing she knew, she was in the hospital.

The emergency room personnel had pumped Tamara's stomach, but she was very sick for three days. When she began to get better, she was transferred to the psychiatric ward of the hospital.

---

*The Psalter is a book of worship, driving us to God by insisting that
we look to Him in the midst of our pain. When we do so, we find
ourselves and our problems absorbed into His bright glory.*

—DAN B. ALLENDER AND TREMPER LONGMAN III, *The Cry of the Soul*

Psychiatric wards are difficult places to see under any circumstances. When your daughter is the patient, the hospital becomes a strange mix of safety and unspeakable horror. I counseled Tamara's mom to see the hospital as a safety net to keep her daughter safe while she marshaled her strength for the continuing fight for Tamara's life. I urged her to let the staff do their job while she got all the support she could.

Marilyn contacted the youth pastor again, who immediately began a prayer chain for her daughter. The youth pastor called and asked me for advice on how to help Tamara. I suggested that he write a letter of love and support to her. I also advised Marilyn to assure Tamara that only I and the youth pastor knew the specifics of her hospital stay and that everyone else was praying for her because they knew that she was ill.

This church did what churches can do best when they are aware and active. Members of the congregation brought food to the family and sent *daily* letters of support and love for over a month. When Tamara came home, she initially felt embarrassed by the attention. Her mom wisely responded, "We can't do this alone. These people love us. We can trust them."

Tamara and her family participated in the outpatient care program the hospital offered, and they incorporated the suggestions into their lives. Tamara continued on medication, and she and her mother both continued counseling with me. Tamara was able to stay current with her schoolwork through home study. The school even sent her assignments home and offered tutoring if needed. Marilyn took a leave of absence from work to stay by Tamara's side. They took walks, went to movies, and tackled a few projects around the house. In other words, they did the hard, daily work of getting better.

Tamara still got agitated and discouraged, and Marilyn got tired—that's why what happened next is so wonderfully relieving. All during Tamara's recovery, her youth pastor prayed for Tamara and prayed specifically for direction as to how the church could participate. When a new intern came to work with the youth group and shared her testimony, the youth pastor knew God was answering his prayers. The intern shared her story with the youth staff about her struggle with depression and suicide attempts when she was a freshman in college.

---

*From [Christ] the whole body, joined and held together
by every supporting ligament, grows and builds itself up in love,
as each part does its work.*

—Ephesians 4:16, NIV

The youth pastor told this young woman about Tamara and asked if he could facilitate their meeting. He called Tamara's mom and asked if he could stop by with something. Tamara and Marilyn assumed it was another casserole. When Tamara opened the door, she was greeted by the youth pastor and the intern. This amazing young woman took courageous initiative and said,

"I know you don't know me, but I want to tell you my story. Can we go somewhere and talk?" Tamara was overwhelmed but too shy to tell her no. As she heard the intern's story, Tamara felt a tiny flicker of hope. *I'm not alone,* she realized.

Tamara and Marilyn's persistent work and the loving support of the church provided a context for Tamara to get better and want to live. Tamara spoke of her healing when she recently told me, "I hope someday I can tell my story to someone and help them!"

Enduring Love

We don't yet see things clearly. We're squinting in a fog, peering through a mist. But it won't be long before the weather clears and the sun shines bright! We'll see it all then, see it all as clearly as God sees us, knowing him directly just as he knows us! But for right now, until that completeness, we have three things to do to lead us toward that consummation: Trust steadily in God, hope unswervingly, love extravagantly. And the best of the three is love.

—1 Corinthians 13:12-13

I *didn't know what to do.* It was three o'clock in the morning, and my infant daughter would not stop crying. I prayed, "God help me." I gently patted Kristin's back, and her cries grew louder. I stepped out of her room for a few minutes, hoping that she would soothe herself, but her cries grew louder still. I looked at the clock. It was 3:15 a.m. I peered out of Kristin's bedroom window into our neighborhood illuminated by a few stars and a flickering streetlight on the corner of our block. It looked as if everyone else in the world was asleep—everyone but my sobbing daughter and me.

I didn't know what to do, so even though it was the middle of the night, I called my mother. "Kristin won't stop crying. I think something is wrong with her. Should I call 911?"

My mother's familiar, calm voice answered on the other end of the telephone line, "Babies cry, Sharon. And sometimes they cry inconsolably. Kristin probably senses that you are anxious about her crying, and that is making her more agitated. Go wrap her in her blanket and rock her in the rocking chair. Maybe you could try singing a lullaby to calm both of you. If she keeps crying, remind yourself that she won't cry forever. There will be many times when what you're doing as a mother will seem like it's not working. Kristin doesn't need you to know what to do all of the time, but she does need to feel your love all of the time."

There were many more crying spells in the wee hours of the morning, and then there were temper tantrums in the middle of the grocery store—and once again, *I didn't know what to do.* There was the Sunday morning when I picked up my beautiful three-year-old from the church nursery, and the nursery worker told me that Kristin would not be able to stay in the nursery until she learned not to hit the other children. *I didn't know what to do.* Was there a support group for mothers of hitting toddlers? Mothers everywhere know the chronology of hurt feelings on the school playground and scraped knees on the soccer field that eventually give way to more hurt feelings in the junior-high-school cafeteria and scraped hearts from not being invited to a slumber party or included with the other girls. So many moments of emotional ups and downs that *I didn't know what to do.*

I was reminded of that 3:00 a.m. crying crisis and my mother's advice just a few weeks ago. Once again it was the middle of the night. Kristin's piercing cries were not keeping me awake. This time it was the deafening silence that kept me tossing and turning, checking the clock every fifteen minutes. Kristin was at her high-school junior-senior prom. Hours earlier she had left home dressed in a beautiful gauzy gown on the arm of a tuxedo-clad boy. He handed her a corsage and escorted her to a limo filled with other girls and boys headed for a fancy restaurant and then to the dance. Kristin left, her eyes filled with stars and her head full of expectations of an enchanted evening. She called me at 9:30 p.m. from the restaurant bathroom. "I spilled spaghetti sauce all down the front of my dress. Andy (her date) isn't talking to me. This night is turning out to be awful. Why does everything have to be so hard? It's just my luck. I hate my life!"

Now I have to tell you that what I wanted to say was "Don't worry, honey. You're too young for fancy restaurants and dances until midnight. I'll come right over and pick you up, and we can go out for ice cream!" Instead I calmly reassured Kristin that all was not lost. I suggested that she find a waiter and ask for some club soda to take out the spaghetti sauce. "Andy is probably nervous too, honey," I consoled. "Just go back out there and be interested in him, and hopefully he'll relax and you'll have a great time. Call me if you need to," and I ended the phone call.

For a few minutes I entertained the fantasy of Kristin calling me again and saying, "Mom, I don't need boys or proms or parties. I just want to be with you. Come and get me." Then I prayed for Kristin and Andy and for the club soda to work and the awkward conversation to become easy.

It was 2:15 a.m. and Kristin was not home yet. You see, after the fancy restaurant and the dance there was *afterprom,* a party at the high school to last until 4:30 a.m.! Who had thought of such a thing? I yearned for the simplicity and safety of my wailing baby daughter in her darkened nursery from years gone by. I couldn't sleep. My mind meandered to my mother's advice more than sixteen years ago: "She doesn't need you to know what to do all of the time, but she does need to know that you love her all of the time."

I had loved her all of the time—that was certain. But not perfectly. I had lost my temper, I had missed meaningful moments, and I had been too controlling at other times. I'd been afraid and unsure. And I'd cried almost as inconsolably as my infant daughter had. I have to admit there were moments when I'd looked at stacks of laundry and piles of homework, or when I'd comforted an emotionally distraught daughter, only to have a new drama develop five minutes later, and I'd murmured, "I hate my life." But I always returned to my mother's anchoring advice: "She just needs you to love her all of the time."

I looked at the clock again, and it was only 3:00 a.m. An hour and a half to wait. I couldn't sleep, so I turned on my bedside lamp and reached for my Bible. I didn't know what I wanted to read, but my Bible automatically fell open to a well-worn passage—a passage I'd turned to in countless times of waiting and wondering and worrying.

A LIGHT IN THE MIDDLE OF THE NIGHT

Second Chronicles 20 tells the story of a small band of God's people in overwhelming circumstances. Jehoshaphat led the people of Judah to follow God and seek His ways, but that didn't mean it was always smooth sailing. In fact, it seemed as if there was one crisis after another. Verse 2 warns of another brewing storm, "Some men came and told Jehoshaphat, 'A vast army is coming against you from Edom, from the other side of the Sea'" (NIV). Jehoshaphat scouted the approaching enemy and cried in distress, "O our God... we have no power to face this vast army that is attacking us. *We do not know what to do*" (verse 12, NIV, emphasis added). Jehoshaphat's fearful plea sounds familiar, doesn't it?

As our daughters enter adolescence and begin to find their way toward adulthood, we see the approaching forces—from within and without. We watch our daughters' moods swing and swirl until we're dizzy, and we see pressures and challenges surrounding them that would prove difficult for a mature person, much less an emotionally immature teenager. We can understand the fear in Jehoshaphat's heart as he surveyed the army surrounding his beloved people. If we look hard enough (especially at three o'clock in the morning), we ourselves can see the surrounding troops of moodiness, peer pressure, depression, the "popular" group at high school, cutting, withdrawal, temptations, suicidal thoughts, conflict, sullenness, and loneliness. "O our God…we have no power to face this vast army that is attacking us. *We do not know what to do.*"

The embattled, anxious King Jehoshaphat leads weary, overwhelmed mothers to light—even in the dark of the middle of the night: "O our God… we have no power to face this vast army that is attacking us. We do not know what to do, *but our eyes are upon you*" (verse 12, NIV, emphasis added). With eyes of faith, Jehoshaphat looked to God and found a way to face the surrounding armies: "Tomorrow march down against them…. Take up your positions; stand firm and see the deliverance the LORD will give you" (verses 16,17, NIV). With a heart of hope, Jehoshaphat calmed his people to see beyond the formidable forces: "Do not be afraid or discouraged because of this vast army. For the battle is not yours, but God's" (verse 15, NIV). And with an unshakable anchor in God's enduring love, Jehoshaphat led his people to rest from their anxious wondering: "Give thanks to the LORD, for his love endures forever" (verse 21, NIV). King Jehoshaphat is a model for mothers who need to find light in the middle of the darkest night.

EYES OF FAITH

I have a friend whose fourteen-year-old daughter is in the midst of teenage turbulence. She swings from hating her life one moment to feeling like the happiest girl in the world the next. She forgets to do her homework. She never forgets to check her e-mail. She's easily annoyed by her brother. She wants to be with her friends all of the time. She suddenly hates the family dog. She wishes she didn't have to go to church anymore. She talks for hours at a time to her best friend. She doesn't have more than a few words to say at dinner.

My friend spends a lot of time staring at grown women. She watches them working in the checkout line at the grocery store or driving alongside her on the freeway. She told me, "I keep telling myself that these functioning members of society were teenage girls once, and they made it!"

My friend's survey of "normal" women is her way of finding faith. We see with the eyes of faith when we "fix our eyes…on what is unseen" (2 Corinthians 4:18, NIV). Never is this truer than for mothering teenage daughters. What is seen is often unpredictable, messy, and even scary. What is unseen, at times, are the girls we know God created our daughters to be—emotionally mature girls with their individual quirkiness and unique giftedness. How do we know? Because what is also unseen but written in our hearts is God's seal of blessing on *us* to be the ones to mother our daughters. We can see what is most true of them, because we know—heart and soul—what is most true of us. We are the ones to mother our daughters through the ups and downs of teenage turbulence.

When we see with eyes of faith a wise Creator who designed each one of us to mother our individual daughters, we see something else, too! We see God's eyes of faith looking back at us. He designed *you* for *your* daughter— He has faith in you! Sometimes we can see this most clearly during the messy days of mothering a daughter toward emotional maturity. Yes, I mean during the *messy* days. When Kristin was about six years old, I left her for the day with a baby-sitter so that I could get a little breather from the tasks of mothering. When I came home, I found a somber daughter and baby-sitter waiting for me. "I'm sorry I was bad," Kristin cried as soon as I walked in the front door.

"What happened?" I asked with my heart beating faster by the moment.

"I'm sorry too," the baby-sitter added as my apprehension grew. "I thought she was playing in her room, but she was writing all over the walls."

My mind flew to the newly painted bedrooms upstairs. "Oh, Kristin," I exclaimed with heartfelt disappointment. "How could you? We just spent a lot of money having the walls painted." And before she could answer, I ran upstairs to survey the damage. "You better come with me," I called angrily to Kristin as I ran up the stairs, "and show me what you've done."

The writing on the bedroom walls stopped me in my tracks. My angry heart quickly melted to a strange mix of guilt for yelling at my daughter and joy for what she had done. Scrawled across the wall in Crayola colors were the words, "My mommy is the best mommy in the world."

God reminds us of our position in the strangest places—in the worry of a late-night vigil, in the ever-changing climate of a teenage girl's moods, in the eagerly scrawled words of a six-year-old. Jehoshaphat's words steady our faith, "Take up your positions; stand firm and see the deliverance the LORD will give you."

Your position: appointed mother to your specially designed daughter. Your mission: to wait for the deliverance God will give you. And while you wait, keep your eyes steadily on Him, and see His faith in you.

A HEART OF HOPE

"Hope is an expectation of receiving, a conviction that there is a way to obtain what we long for."[1] Jehoshaphat's heart of hope was enlivened and steadied by his dialogue with God. After Jehoshaphat learned of the overwhelming battle ahead, he prayed, "O LORD, God of our fathers, are you not the God who is in heaven?… If calamity comes upon us, whether the sword of judgment, or plague or famine, we will stand in your presence before this temple that bears your Name and will cry out to you in our distress, and you will hear us and save us" (2 Chronicles 20:6,9, NIV).

The avenue of hope for Jehoshaphat was his petition to God. His fearful heart began to beat steadily with hope after he laid his heart bare before God. Then he remembered, "the battle is not [ours], but God's" (verse 15, NIV).

Your daughter is not yours, she is God's—given by Him to you to mother, to love, and to lead toward emotional maturity. Daily make your requests for her known to God. Describe the challenges. Tell Him about the moodiness, the depression, and the ups and downs of her life and yours. And then leave her in His hands. What exactly does that mean, leave her in His hands? I have heard wise mothers talk about visualizing leaving their daughters in the arms of God. I have heard more pragmatic mothers talk about writing down their requests on a piece of paper, presenting it to God, and tearing it up to symbolize that the requests are now in His hands. These are good ideas to make the surrender of our children to God more tangible. But I think leaving our children in His hands has more to do with hope.

When I remember Kristin is God's, my heart cannot help but be filled with hope—hope in His creation, His wisdom, His creativity, His longsuffering, His heart for my daughter. And as I come to Him, heart in my hands, I see His hope in me. I get discouraged, angry, and overwhelmed. And He whispers, "Do not be afraid or discouraged. This battle is not yours, but mine." I whine, pout, and complain. And He answers, "Do not be afraid or discouraged. This battle is not yours, but mine."

I tell Him about Kristin's moodiness, her hurtful words, and her emotional aches and pains. And He tells me over and over again words of hope for both Kristin and me: "Do not be afraid or discouraged. This daughter is not yours, but mine!" Hope unswervingly in Him and discover His hope in you.

AN ANCHOR IN GOD'S ENDURING LOVE

Before the battle had even begun, Jehoshaphat reminded his people of its sure ending:

> "Listen to me, Judah and people of Jerusalem! Have faith in the LORD
> your God and you will be upheld; have faith in his prophets and you
> will be successful."…[and] they went out at the head of the army, say-
> ing: "Give thanks to the LORD, for his love endures forever." (2 Chron-
> icles 20:20-21, NIV)

Somehow knowing of God's enduring love gave courage, fortitude, and eventually, victory. This Old Testament story reminds me of my mother's advice in the wee hours of the morning that somehow my love for my daughter would get me through the night and the nights to come.

Some of you may be in a dark night of mothering right now, and you wonder where the truth in this is for you. After all, not every mothering story ends in victory. I have learned about mothering in the midst of heartbreaking sorrow from my own mother. My mother went through an unspeakably difficult time when my brother was on drugs. I will never forget the day when my mother had to decide whether to press charges against her own son for stealing from her checking account to buy cocaine. The choice was agonizing: either continue to protect him from the consequences of his actions, or sentence him to an arrest warrant. We didn't know where my brother was.

I stood by my mother as the tears ran down both our faces and she signed the papers. Then she did the strangest thing; she took the pen and started writing on her hand. I asked, "What are you writing?"

"I'm writing the number for his arrest warrant," she answered. "It's all I know about him right now."

My mind immediately went to that Old Testament scripture, "Can a mother forget the baby at her breast and have no compassion on the child she has borne? Though she may forget, I will not forget you! See, I have engraved you on the palms of my hands" (Isaiah 49:15-16, NIV).

Mothering invites us to participate in the fellowship of His sufferings and compels us to believe that there is One who writes *our* names on the palm of His hands.

The New Testament affirms that when we remember God's love for us, we will be able to love. The apostle John wrote eloquently, "We...are going to love—love and be loved. First we were loved, now we love. He loved us first" (1 John 4:19).

My mother was right. There have been countless times when I have not known what to do, but I can love. The wondrous circle of the give-and-take of extravagant love is this: As I love my daughter, I experience more of God's love for me, and as I experience God's love for me, I can better love my daughter. God does not leave us in the dark as to what this love looks like— neither His love for us nor our love for our daughters. He fleshes out love in one of the most well-known passages in Scripture: 1 Corinthians 13.

A few weeks ago Kristin helped me as I wrote my paraphrase of 1 Corinthians 13, a "mothering" version of these inspired words that arose out of our journey together in the emotional ups and downs of her adolescent years. I conclude with these words in hopes that they will inspire you to make this familiar passage of Scripture *incarnational.* Let it live and move and take shape in your own journey with your daughter toward emotional maturity. "We have three things to do to lead us toward that consummation: Trust steadily in God, hope unswervingly, love extravagantly. And the best of the three is love" (1 Corinthians 13:13).

1 Corinthians 13 for Mothers of Teenage Girls

Love is patient. Love never gives up, even after saying eleven times, "Please tell me what's wrong."

Love is kind. Love cares more for my daughter than I do for a clean house, a full bank account, or a quiet evening curled up with a good book.

It does not envy. Love doesn't want my daughter to be like any other girl in the world. Love wants her to be exactly who she is.

It does not boast. Love doesn't say, "I told you so" (even though I did tell her that she would be tired and irritable if she stayed up until 4:30 a.m.!).

It is not proud. Love doesn't take credit for her accomplishments—they are all hers!

It is not rude. Love doesn't expect her to dress like me, act like me, or be interested in the same things I am.

It is not self-seeking. Love isn't always pushing her own agenda. Love lets her find her own way.

It is not easily angered. Love doesn't yell, "Don't you take that tone with me, young lady."

It keeps no record of wrongs. Love doesn't keep score of the times she came in late, didn't clean her room, or slammed her bedroom door.

Love does not delight in evil. Love hurts when she hurts and rejoices when she is glad.

But rejoices with the truth. Love takes pleasure in waiting for her timing, her growth, and her emotional maturity as if watching the delicate unfolding of a beautiful, blooming rose.

It always protects. Love puts up with sulking, crying, yelling, pouting, whining, and complaining.

Always trusts. Love remembers that she is God's child—a magnificent loan for a while, but she is His.

Always hopes. Love always looks for the creative, beautiful, amazing girl behind the unpredictable, messy, moody facade.

Always perseveres. Love listens to her daughter's lament, "Mom, I hate my life!" and sees a chance to begin again, make new trust again, forgive again, and demonstrate again that undergirding her relationship with her daughter is a commitment that the greatest earthquake cannot shake.

Love never fails. Love keeps going toward emotional maturity, unwilling to trade this difficult, demanding, and infinitely rewarding journey for anything!

FINDING CAREGIVERS
FOR YOUR DAUGHTER

As you walk hand in hand with your daughter through the ups and downs of her emotional development, both of you may need to talk with a counselor. The best counseling will not replace your relationship with your daughter but will enhance it by providing insight and guidance to strengthen your alliance. Listed below are some tips for finding the best counselor and some suggestions in the event that insurance or income is not available to cover the costs of counseling.

FINDING A PHYSICIAN

- Don't assume that all physicians understand adolescent depression and its treatment. Interview your doctor and ask how he or she addresses teenage depression. Many pediatricians and adolescent physicians are not comfortable prescribing antidepressants and may refer your daughter to a psychiatrist after seeing her. Your daughter will probably not be happy about having to see two doctors. Interview and ask questions to streamline the process so that your daughter only sees the person who is likely to be the most helpful.
- If you first see a general psychiatrist or a psychiatrist who specializes in working with adolescents, interview him or her as well. Match the doctor's style with your daughter's personality. Give as much background in your initial meeting as possible so that the doctor will know what's going on even if your daughter is not being especially communicative. Ask the doctor to explain the rationale behind the medication he or she chooses for your daughter, including its potential side effects and how to evaluate its effectiveness.
- You will need to be as informed a consumer as possible. Read about antidepressants (see resources section on page 209) and what effective treatment for depression looks like. Unfortunately, sometimes it takes a few tries with medications (and doctors and therapists) to get the

right fit. Antidepressants are most effective when the patient is self-aware and can evaluate how well they are working. You will have to observe your daughter very closely to help her evaluate this, since she may not be self-aware. Don't be afraid to tell the doctor what you think your daughter needs based on your own research and observations. A mother's intuition counts for at least as much as a formal education!

- Antidepressants work best in conjunction with therapy. The suggestions in the following section can help you find a therapist. However, you will be the best judge of whether you've found a good therapist for your daughter. As important as knowledge and experience is finding someone whose personality works with your daughter's personality and who is respectful of what you know as well as your questions and concerns. Good therapy can take time, and that can be scary when you are in a crisis. You will be able to trust the process if you find someone who is knowledgeable, honors you and your daughter, and expresses a commitment to find out what he or she does not know— all of which is a somewhat subjective experience that you will have to prayerfully evaluate.

FINDING A THERAPIST

- The best therapist referrals come from those who have been through a similar struggle. If you don't know of anyone whose daughter has struggled with emotional development or depression, contact youth pastors and school counselors, and ask them if they can help you locate someone who has sought professional help for their daughter.
- Contact your insurance company for a list of providers and information about the number of sessions they will pay for and how much they will pay.
- Interview at least three therapists (with your daughter) before choosing one. It is important that your daughter feel that she is part of the process of choosing who will help her. Just as with finding a physician, you may need to interview first and weed out therapists who you're certain won't be a good fit for your daughter.

- Choose a therapist whose work focuses on adolescents and their emotional development. I recommend female counselors for teenage girls. Although there are many good male therapists who specialize in working with teens, adolescent girls are more likely to deal honestly and openly with their issues if they are working with a female counselor.
- When you interview the therapist, explain that you want to be involved in your daughter's recovery, and ask the therapist how he or she will incorporate you into the process. Interview to get a sense of the responsiveness of the therapist to what you already know and have experienced.
- If insurance is not available and money is tight, ask about a sliding scale. Many therapists will adjust their fees to accommodate your income.
- Ask your church about a counseling support fund. Often a church will pay half of the counseling fee, while you pay the other half.
- If counseling is out of the question due to your financial situation, look for a support group in your community. Investigate and interview group leaders as carefully as you would a therapist.
- Contact the National Mental Health Association Information Center at 1-800-969-NMHA for referrals to local support groups and community resources.
- Check with your local hospital about educational meetings on adolescent emotional development.

RESOURCES

The following resources may not reflect all of your beliefs and values. I have listed them as a source of information, but they should be reviewed and evaluated before you decide to make them available to your daughter.

FEMALE DEVELOPMENT

The Girls' Life Guide to Growing Up. Karen Bokram and Alexis Sinex. Hillsboro, OR: Beyond Words, 2000.

Girltalk: All the Stuff Your Sister Never Told You. Carol Weston. New York: HarperTrade, 1997.

It's Perfectly Normal: Changing Bodies, Growing Up, Sex, and Sexual Health. Robie H. Harris. Cambridge, MA: Candlewick Press, 1996.

Odd Girl Out: The Hidden Culture of Aggression in Girls. Rachel Simmons. New York: Harcourt Trade, 2003.

Queen Bees and Wannabes: Helping Your Daughter Survive Cliques, Gossip, Boyfriends, and Other Realities of Adolescence. Rosalind Wiseman. New York: Crown Publishing, 2003.

"Trust Me, Mom—Everyone Else Is Going!" The New Rules for Mothering Adolescent Girls. Roni Cohen-Sandler. New York: Penguin Group, Viking Penguin, 2002.

Other Resources

Brio magazine. Available from Focus on the Family: 1-800-A-FAMILY.

MOTHERING

Different Children, Different Needs. Charles F. Boyd. Sisters, OR: Multnomah, 2003.

"I'm Not Mad, I Just Hate You!" A New Understanding of Mother-Daughter Conflict. Roni Cohen-Sandler and Michelle Silver. New York: Penguin Group, 2000.

Keep Talking: A Mother-Daughter Guide to the Pre-Teen Years. Lynda Madison. Kansas City, MO: Andrews and McMeel, 1999.

Reviving Ophelia: Saving the Selves of Adolescent Girls. Mary Pipher. New York: Ballantine Books, 1999.

YOUTH CULTURE

Living in the Image Culture: An Introductory Primer for Media Literacy Education. Francis Davis. Los Angeles, CA: Center for Media and Values, 1992.
Understanding Today's Youth Culture. Walt Mueller. Wheaton, IL: Tyndale, 1999.

Other Resources
Center for Media Literacy
3101 Ocean Park Boulevard, #200
Santa Monica, CA 90405
310-581-0260
Fax: 310-581-0270
1-800-226-9494
www.medialit.org

The Center for Parent/Youth Understanding Newsletter
PO Box 414
Elizabethtown, PA 17022
717-361-0031
www.cpyu.org

BODY IMAGE

Everything You Need to Know About Body Dysmorphic Disorder: Dealing with a Distorted Body Image. Pamela Walker. New York: Rosen Publishing, 1999.
The Pursuit of Beauty: Finding Beauty That Will Last Forever. Katie Luce. Green Forest, AR: New Leaf Press, 1998.
Transforming Body Image: Learning to Love the Body You Have. Edited by Marcia Germaine Hutchinson. Santa Cruz, CA: Crossing Press, 1985.
What's Real, What's Ideal: Overcoming a Negative Body Image. Brangien Davis. Center City, MN: Hazelden Publishing and Educational Services, 1999.

Other Resources
Body Talk. A twenty-eight-minute video on body acceptance. Order from Body Positive: 2417 Prospect St., A, Berkeley, CA 94704; 510-841-9389.

Building Blocks for Children's Body Image. Marius Griffin. From the Body
Image Task Force: PO Box 360196, Melbourne, FL 32936; http://
home.earthlink.net/~dawn_atkins/bitf.htm.

HEALTHY EATING

*American Academy of Pediatrics Guide to Your Child's Nutrition: Making Peace at
the Table and Building Healthy Eating Habits for Life.* William H. Dietz and
Lorraine Stern. New York: Random House, Villard, 1999.

The American Diabetes Association Guide to Healthy Restaurant Eating. Hope S.
Warshaw. Alexandria, VA: American Diabetes Association, 1998.

Eating on the Run. Evelyn Tribole. Champaign, IL: Human Kinetics,
2003.

Eating Well in a Busy World. Francine Allen. Berkeley, CA: Ten Speed Press,
1986.

*Like Mother, Like Daughter: How Women Are Influenced by Their Mothers' Rela-
tionship with Food—And How to Break the Pattern.* Debra Waterhouse.
Collingdale, PA: DIANE Publishing, 1999.

Making Peace with Food: Freeing Yourself from the Diet/Weight Obsession. Susan
Kano. New York: HarperPerennial, 1989.

*Outsmarting the Female Fat Cell: The First Weight-Control Program Designed
Specifically for Women.* Debra Waterhouse. New York: Warner Books,
1994.

Preventing Childhood Eating Problems. Jane R. Hirschmann and Lela Zaphiro-
poulos. Carlsbad, CA: Gurze Books, 1993.

EATING DISORDERS

Hope, Help, and Healing for Eating Disorders. Gregory L. Jantz, PhD. Colorado
Springs: Shaw Books, 2002.

*Life Inside the "Thin" Cage: A Personal Look into the Hidden World of the Chronic
Dieter.* Constance Rhodes. Colorado Springs: WaterBrook, Shaw Books,
2003.

*"Mom, I Feel Fat!" Becoming Your Daughter's Ally in Developing a Healthy Body
Image.* Sharon A. Hersh. Colorado Springs: WaterBrook, Shaw Books,
2001.

When Food's a Foe: How to Confront and Conquer Eating Disorders. Nancy J.
Kolodny. Madison, WI: Turtleback Books, 1992.

Other Resources
National Eating Disorders Association
603 Stewart Street, Suite 803
Seattle, WA 98101
206-382-3587
www.nationaleatingdisorders.org

Remuda Ranch, Center for Anorexia and Bulimia
PO Box 2481
Wickenburg, AZ 85390
1-800-445-1900
info@remudaranch.com

ANOREXIA
The Golden Cage: The Enigma of Anorexia Nervosa. Hilde Bruch. Cambridge,
    MA: Harvard University Press, 2001.
*Little Girls in Pretty Boxes: The Making and Breaking of Elite Gymnasts and Figure
    Skaters.* Joan Ryan. New York: Warner Books, 2000.
Stick Figure: A Diary of My Former Self. Lori Gottlieb. New York: Berkley Pub-
    lishing Group, 2001.

Other Resources
Information on obtaining the 1997 television movie based on the book *Little
Girls in Pretty Boxes* can be found at www.lifetimetv.com.

National Association of Anorexia Nervosa and Associated Disorders
Highland Hospital
718 Glenview Avenue
Highland Park, IL 60035
847-432-8000

BULIMIA
Bulimia: A Guide to Recovery. Lindsey Hall and Leigh Cohn. Carlsbad, CA:
    Gurze Books, 1999.
Wasted: A Memoir of Anorexia and Bulimia. Marya Hornbacher. New York:
    HarperCollins, 1999.

Other Resources
American Anorexia/Bulimia Association
293 Central Park West, Suite 1R
New York, NY 10024
212-501-8351

The following movies are still shown periodically on television. You can find out when they might be shown at www.eonline.com/facts/movies.

Dying to Be Perfect: The Ellen Hart Pena Story. ABC, 1996.
For the Love of Nancy. Lifetime, 1994. Information at www.lifetimetv.com.
Kate's Secret. Lifetime, 1986. Information at www.lifetimetv.com.

COMPULSIVE OVEREATING
The Overweight Child: Promoting Fitness and Self-Esteem. Teresa Pitman and
    Miriam Kaufman. New York: Firefly Books, 2000.
Why Weight? A Guide to Ending Compulsive Eating. Geneen Roth. New York:
    Dutton/Plume, 1989.

Other Resources
Amplestuff: Everything for Big People (except clothes). Catalog with larger sizes. PO
    Box 116, Bearsville, NY 12409; 914-679-3316; www.amplestuff.com.

National Center for Overcoming Overeating
PO Box 1257, Old Chelsea Station
New York, NY 10113-0920
212-875-0442

CUTTING
Bodily Harm: The Breakthrough Healing Program for Self-Injurers. Karen Con-
    terio and Wendy Lader. New York: Hyperion, 1999.
Cutting: Understanding and Overcoming Self-Mutilation. Steven Levenkron. New
    York: W. W. Norton & Company, 1999.
Secret Scars: Uncovering and Understanding the Addiction of Self-Injury. V. J.
    Turner. Center City, MN: Hazelden Publishing and Educational Services,
    2002.

Other Resources
Self Abuse Finally Ends (SAFE); 1-800-DONT CUT (1-800-366-8288);
     www.safe-alternatives.com.

www.cyberinfo.com/selfharm/htm.

DEPRESSION

Depression Is the Pits, but I'm Getting Better: A Guide for Adolescents. E. Jane
     Garland. Washington, DC: American Psychological Association,
     1998.
Depression: What It Is, How to Beat It. Linda Wasmer Smith. Berkeley Heights,
     NJ: Enslow Publishers, 2000.
*"Help Me, I'm Sad": Recognizing, Treating and Preventing Childhood and
     Adolescent Depression.* David G. Fassler. New York: Penguin Group, 1998.
Lonely, Sad and Angry: How to Help Your Hurting Child. Barbara D. Ingersoll
     and Sam Goldstein. Plantation, FL: Specialty Press, 2001.
More Than Moody: Recognizing and Treating Adolescent Depression. Harold S.
     Koplewicz. New York: Penguin Group, 2002.
Moving Beyond Depression: A Whole-Person Approach to Healing. Gregory L.
     Jantz, PhD. Colorado Springs: Shaw Books, 2003.
Overcoming Teen Depression: A Guide for Parents. Miriam Kaufman. New York:
     Firefly Books, 2001.
Teen Torment: Overcoming Verbal Abuse at Home and at School. Patricia Evans.
     Avon, MA: Adams Media, 2003.
Understanding Weight and Depression: A Teen Eating Disorder Prevention Book.
     Julie M. Clarke and Ann Kirby-Payne. New York: Rosen Publishing, 2000.
When Nothing Matters Anymore: A Survival Guide for Depressed Teens. Bev
     Cobain and Elizabeth Verdick. Minneapolis: Free Spirit Publishing, 1998.

Other Resources
Child and Adolescent Bipolar Foundation
www.cabf.org

Depression and Bipolar Support Alliance
730 North Franklin Street, Suite 501

Chicago, IL 60610

1-800-826-3632

www.dbsalliance.org

SUICIDE

Dare to Live: A Guide to the Understanding and Prevention of Teenage Suicide and Depression. Michael Miller. Hillsboro, OR: Beyond Words Publishing, 1989.

Fatal Choice: The Teenage Suicide Crisis. John Q. Baucom. Chicago: Moody Publishers, 1987.

Night Falls Fast: Understanding Suicide. Kay Redfield Jamison. Collingdale, PA: DIANE Publishing, 2003.

Other Resources

American Foundation for Suicide Prevention

120 Wall Street, 22nd Floor

New York, NY 10005

1-888-333-2377

www.afsp.org

Suicide Prevention Action Network USA, Inc.

PO Box 73368

Washington, DC 20056-3368

1-888-649-1366

Fax: 202-387-3187

info@spanusa.org

NOTES

INTRODUCTION: A HAVEN IN THE STORM

1. From U.S. Department of Justice, *Bureau of Justice Statistics, 2002* (Washington, DC: Government Printing Office, 2002), NCJ 194449. Found at www.ojp.usdoj.gov/bjs.

CHAPTER 1: BEING A MOM IS NOT FOR THE FAINT OF HEART

1. Harville Hendrix and Helen Hunt, *Giving the Love That Heals: A Guide for Parents* (New York: Simon & Schuster, Atria Books, 1997), 156.
2. From T. Berry Brazelton and Bertrand G. Cramer, *The Earliest Relationship: Parents, Infants and the Drama of Early Attachment* (Reading, MA: Addison-Wesley Longman, 1990).
3. Hendrix and Hunt, *Giving the Love That Heals,* 33.
4. Martha Tod Dudman, *Augusta, Gone: A True Story* (New York: Simon & Schuster, 2001), 15-17.

CHAPTER 2: BECOMING AN ALLY—USING DIFFICULTIES TO BUILD A RELATIONSHIP

1. Mary Pipher, *Reviving Ophelia: Saving the Selves of Adolescent Girls* (New York: Ballantine, 1994), 281.
2. Pipher, *Reviving Ophelia,* 281.
3. Pipher, *Reviving Ophelia,* 281.

CHAPTER 3: BEING A TEENAGE GIRL IS NOT EASY

1. Anne Moir, *Brain Sex: The Real Difference Between Men and Women* (New York: Dell Publishing, 1991), 33-37.
2. Daniel Goleman, *Emotional Intelligence: Why It Can Matter More Than IQ* (New York: Bantam Books, 1997), 81-82.
3. Peggy Patten, "Living with Adolescents: An Interview with Reed Larson," *Parent News* (January/February 2000): 2.
4. From Gesele Lajoie, Alyson McLellan, and Cindi Seddon, *Take Action Against Bullying* (Coquitlam, BC: Bully B'ware Productions, 1997), 49.

5. From Nan Stein, Nancy L. Marshall, and Linda R. Tropp, *Secrets in Public: Sexual Harassment in Our Schools—A Report on the Results of a* Seventeen *Magazine Survey* (Wellesley, MA: Wellesley College Center for Research on Women, 1993), 7.

CHAPTER 4: BECOMING AN ALLY—MOVING TOWARD
EMOTIONAL MATURITY

1. Hugh Prather, *Spiritual Notes to Myself: Essential Wisdom for the 21st Century* (York Beach, ME: Red Wheel/Weiser, 1998), 62.

2. Patricia Evans, *Teen Torment: Overcoming Verbal Abuse at Home and at School* (Avon, MA: Adams Media, 2003), 70.

3. Dan Allender, *The Healing Path: How the Hurts in Your Past Can Lead You to a More Abundant Life* (Colorado Springs: WaterBrook, 1999), 15.

4. Prather, *Spiritual Notes to Myself,* 65.

CHAPTER 5: "MOM, I'M NOT IN THE MOOD!"

1. Mary Pipher, *Reviving Ophelia: Saving the Selves of Adolescent Girls* (New York: Ballantine, 1994), 281.

2. From Anne Moir, *Brain Sex: The Real Difference Between Men and Women* (New York: Dell Publishing, 1991), 33-37.

3. From Doug Milman, *Are You Normal? Lunacy Defined and Profusely Illustrated* (New York: HarperCollins, 1984), 17.

4. Thomas Merton, *Thoughts in Solitude* (New York: Farrar, Straus & Giroux, 1956), 72.

CHAPTER 6: "MOM, JUST LEAVE ME ALONE!"

1. Nicki R. Crick et al., "Childhood Aggression and Gender: A New Look at an Old Problem," in *Gender and Motivation,* ed. Dan Bernstein (Lincoln, NE: University of Nebraska Press, 1999), 4.

2. Sharon A. Hersh, *Bravehearts: Unlocking the Courage to Love with Abandon* (Colorado Springs: WaterBrook, 2000), 8-9.

CHAPTER 7: "MOM, I'M SO STRESSED OUT!"

1. Geoffrey Cowley, "Our Bodies, Our Fears," *Newsweek* (24 February 2003): 44.

2. From Cowley, "Our Bodies, Our Fears," 48.

3. Kristin's teacher gave her students an assignment to write a poem answering the question "What if...?" Kristin's poem is typical of the expressions of junior-high anxiety. Used by permission of Kristin Hersh.

4. From Cowley, "Our Bodies, Our Fears," 47.

5. Dr. Bruce Perry, quoted in Archibald Hart, *Adrenaline and Stress: The Exciting New Breakthrough That Helps You Overcome Stress Damage* (Dallas: Word, 1995), 48.

6. George Howe Colt and Anne Hollister, quoted in Daniel G. Amen, *Change Your Brain, Change Your Life: The Breakthrough Program for Conquering Anxiety, Depression, Obsessiveness, Anger, and Impulsiveness* (New York: Three Rivers Publishing, 1998), 74.

CHAPTER 8: "MOM, EVERYONE HATES ME!"

1. Rosalind Wiseman, *Queen Bees and Wannabes: Helping Your Daughter Survive Cliques, Gossip, Boyfriends, and Other Realities of Adolescence* (New York: Three Rivers Press, 2002), 173.

CHAPTER 9: EATING DISORDERS

1. Mary Pipher, *Hunger Pains: The Modern Woman's Tragic Quest for Thinness* (Holbrook, MA: Adams Publishing, 1995), 53.

2. Quoted in Lori Gottlieb, "I Had an Eating Disorder and Didn't Even Know It!" *CosmoGirl* (April 2001): 149.

3. From Margery D. Rosen, "Is Your Child Headed for an Eating Disorder?" *Child* (August 2000): 62.

4. Kathryn J. Zerbe, *The Body Betrayed: Women, Eating Disorders, and Treatment* (Carlsbad, CA: Gurze Books, 1995), 168.

CHAPTER 10: CUTTING AND SELF-INJURY

1. From Karen Conterio and Wendy Lader, *Bodily Harm: The Breakthrough Healing Program for Self-Injurers* (New York: Hyperion, 1998), 7.

2. Conterio and Lader, *Bodily Harm,* 21-22.

3. From Dora Bide, "Skin Deep: A Story of Secret Cutting," *Teen People* (January 2001): 60.

4. Conterio and Lader, *Bodily Harm,* 16.

5. From Bide, "Skin Deep," 60.
6. From Bide, "Skin Deep," 60.
7. Conterio and Lader, *Bodily Harm,* 7.
8. Conterio and Lader, *Bodily Harm,* 164.
9. This poem was quoted by permission.

CHAPTER 11: DEPRESSION

1. Miriam Kaufman, *Overcoming Teen Depression: A Guide for Parents* (New York: Firefly Books, 2001), 6.
2. From Kaufman, *Overcoming Teen Depression,* 2.
3. From Kaufman, *Overcoming Teen Depression,* 46.
4. Jane Kenyon, "Having It Out with Melancholy," quoted in *Unholy Ghost: Writers on Depression,* ed. Nell Casey (New York: Morrow, 2001), 6.
5. Harriet Lerner, *The Mother Dance: How Children Change Your Life* (New York: HarperPerennial, 1998), 76-77.
6. Gregory Jantz, PhD, *Moving Beyond Depression: A Whole-Person Approach to Healing* (Colorado Springs: Shaw Books, 2003), 1.
7. From Gabriel Cousens and Mark Mayell, *Depression-Free for Life: An All-Natural, Five-Step Plan to Reclaim Your Zest for Life* (New York: HarperCollins, 2000).
8. Kaufman, *Overcoming Teen Depression,* 52.
9. From Kaufman, *Overcoming Teen Depression,* 7.
10. From Kaufman, *Overcoming Teen Depression,* 8.

CHAPTER 12: SUICIDE

1. Kay Redfield Jamison, *Night Falls Fast: Understanding Suicide* (New York: Vintage Books, 1999), 34.
2. From Miriam Kaufman, *Overcoming Teen Depression: A Guide for Parents* (New York: Firefly Books, 2001), 190-92.
3. From Edwin Shneidman, *Definition of Suicide* (New York: John Wiley & Sons, 1985), 21.
4. From P. A. Carlton and F. P. Deanne, "Impact of Attitudes and Suicidal Ideation on Adolescents' Intentions to Seek Professional Psychiatric Help," *Journal of Adolescence* (2000): 23, 35-45.

5. Jamison, *Night Falls Fast,* 38.

6. Jamison, *Night Falls Fast,* 236.

CONCLUSION: ENDURING LOVE

1. Sharon A. Hersh, *Bravehearts: Unlocking the Courage to Love with Abandon* (Colorado Springs: WaterBrook, 2000), 174.

ABOUT THE AUTHOR

SHARON HERSH is a licensed professional counselor and the mother of two teenagers. She is the author of *"Mom, I Feel Fat!" Becoming Your Daughter's Ally in Developing a Healthy Body Image* and *Bravehearts: Unlocking the Courage to Love with Abandon*. A sought-after speaker for retreats and conferences, Sharon lives with her family in Lone Tree, Colorado.

Learn How You Can Use
Hand-in-Hand Mothering Skills
to Become the *Ally*
Your Daughter Needs.

Hand-in-hand mothering is… responding to your daughter not out of insecurity or fear, but out of a limitless love for her. It is a way of mothering that is filled with hope, as every struggle, question, and failure becomes an opportunity for transformation—for you and your daughter.

WATERBROOK PRESS
www.waterbrookpress.com